# Changing Churches

Blessings,
Dottie Parish

# Changing Churches

## A View From the Pew

Dottie Parish

WinePress Publishing
Great Books, Defined.

ISBN 13: 978-1-4141-2152-9
ISBN 10: 1-4141-2152-0
Library of Congress Catalog Card Number: 2011933365

# Contents

Introduction . . . . . . . . . . . . . . . . . . . . . . . . . . . . . . . . . vii

**Part 1: A Journey In Three Churches . . . . . . . . . . . . . . . 1**
Two Types of Change

1. A Faith Journey . . . . . . . . . . . . . . . . . . . . . . . . . . . 3
2. Strange Teachings. . . . . . . . . . . . . . . . . . . . . . . . . . 14
3. Loss, Looking, and Leaving . . . . . . . . . . . . . . . . . . . . 21
4. A Big Surprise Church . . . . . . . . . . . . . . . . . . . . . . . 27
5. Too Many Spectacular Changes . . . . . . . . . . . . . . . . . 35
6. Struggling, Searching, and Leaving . . . . . . . . . . . . . . 43
7. A Smaller Church, Big Surprise . . . . . . . . . . . . . . . . . 53

**Interlude: Guide for Leavers and Leaders. . . . . . . . . . . 62**
Tears and Reason

**Part 2: Lessons For Changing Churches . . . . . . . . . . . . 81**
Get Ready

8. Ideas for the Sheep. . . . . . . . . . . . . . . . . . . . . . . . . 83
9. Ideas for the Shepherds . . . . . . . . . . . . . . . . . . . . . . 91

10. Worthy Worship . . . . . . . . . . . . . . . . . . . . . . . . . . . . 100
11. Christ-Like Makeovers . . . . . . . . . . . . . . . . . . . . . . . . . 113
12. Go and Tell, Go and Help . . . . . . . . . . . . . . . . . . . . . . 126
13. Changing Churches in a Changing Culture . . . . . . . 143
14. Transforming Churches . . . . . . . . . . . . . . . . . . . . . . . . 162

Acknowledgments . . . . . . . . . . . . . . . . . . . . . . . . . . . . . 171

Endnotes . . . . . . . . . . . . . . . . . . . . . . . . . . . . . . . . . . 173

# Introduction

THE OUTLINE FOR *Changing Churches* dropped into my mind during my quiet time—utterly surprising me. *Should I write about such personal matters? Would this glorify God?* Over a period of months I prayed about it, asking God's guidance. I realized others could benefit from learning about my journey. I hope my experiences will speak to:

- Christians going through similar struggles when leaving a church or upset over friends leaving a church.
- Christians who can't understand why anyone leaves a church or who think they would never leave a church.
- Pastors and church leaders ministering to members who are dissatisfied or preparing to leave.
- Pastors and church leaders welcoming visitors who are grieving the loss of their former church and going through the interesting but difficult search for a new church.
- All of us, helping us understand what we need to do to build up the body, the church, the bride of Christ.

Though this is my story, God is the main character and the star of the story. He and his Word guided my way. I hope readers will keep this in mind and be amazed by him. This is also my husband, Mike's, story. We traveled this road together. You will hear some of the ways we differed, though I tell the story from my own point of view. He lovingly supported this project, reading the manuscript and helping edit it. We are a team.

Mike and I are very loyal. We commit wholeheartedly to friends, groups, and organizations. We do this especially with the church because we believe God directs our steps and it's not up to us to "decide" to leave a church. We couldn't comprehend God directing us to leave not one, but two churches. He surprised us! I hope sharing our experiences gives readers insight into

- The right reasons to leave a church.
- The pain and angst involved in leaving a familiar church.
- The search for another church and the problems this entails.
- The discord between spouses about leaving a church and finding another church.
- Finding the new church that fits you and fits God's plan for you.

Did God direct Abraham to leave? Did God tell Jonah to go to another place? We should not be surprised when he moves us. Sometimes God shakes us up in one church and leads us to another church as a way of stretching us, taking us out of our comfort zones. Sometimes God moves us from one church to another to use us in the new location.

Part 1 details our journey in three churches: the struggles, the prayers, the searches, and the amazing answers to prayers. The three churches described in this book are like three friends—each playing a different part in our journey. All friends have flaws, and no two are alike. The same is true for churches. In describing each church, it's difficult to avoid implied criticisms and comparisons. Just as friends cannot be compared to one another, neither can churches. Each is unique and distinct. I hope readers will see the goodness in each church and not exaggerate or dwell on the flaws.

The names of churches and individuals have been changed to protect their identity. I include excerpts from my journals, letters, and e-mails (to two of my pastors), and thoughts from extensive reading. Our return to church in 1990 is included to help readers understand the scope of what God has done.

An interlude between part 1 and part 2 gives a manual for understanding church leavers and a road map for navigating the struggle and grief in switching churches.

Part 2 is a primer on church life educating readers about the ways churches have and are changing. Our story and the wisdom of experts weave throughout, giving information about the seeker church and the emerging church, about pragmatism, narcissism, and relativism in our culture and in the church. The need for church unity, correct teaching, and commitment are stressed.

Part 2 also offers solutions to return the church to faith and unity. These aren't easy or quick answers. But they are proven biblical solutions involving discipleship, growing, healing, and holding accountable. We must confess our sin, repent, and change directions. We must be transformed. We must be witnesses and servants living the "love one another" Scriptures.

In spite of a lack of unity, in spite of apathy, and in spite of changes in the church, God has used faithful Christians through the ages to build his church. I believe there are some faith-filled men and women in every Christian church who keep the flame of Christ's love burning. They know that Jesus is the Christ and the solid foundation stone of the church. "And the gates of hell shall not prevail against it" (Matt. 16:18 ESV). We are on an exciting journey and hope to take you along to learn from what we have learned.

Church ... unity comes not from organization or ritual or liturgy; it comes from Christ.... Where Christ is, there is the church. The church will realize her unity only when she realizes that she does not exist to propagate the point of view of any body of men, but to provide a home where the Spirit of Christ can dwell and where all men who love Christ can meet in that Spirit.

—William Barclay

## Part 1

# A Journey In Three Churches

## Two Types of Change

As FOURTH GRADERS we watch a caterpillar spinning its cocoon. We inspect the cocoon every day. The days creep by. The teacher claims vast unseen changes are happening; we must give nature time. Finally the day comes. We watch in stunned silence as a butterfly struggles and emerges. Its brilliant orange and black wings dazzle our eyes. What an amazing change! What a transformation!

Decades later, the author watches a neatly kept, well-established neighborhood change in a different way. It's called eminent domain. By law, homes are taken from people, and decent neighborhoods are destroyed to make way for commercial progress—for the sake of economic benefit. Some changes are beautiful. Some are destructive.

This book explores two types of church change, man-devised versus God-led; pragmatic versus prayerful; eminent domain versus transformation. There have always been changes in churches, and there should be. Change is necessary for growth. Without change we're in a rut; we're stagnant. Without change we die. Local church "makeovers" devised by men rather than designed by God are what I term "eminent domain" changes. It's a metaphor, not an exact description. I use it to wake up the church, all of us, to the misguided nature of some church changes.

Jesus said, "On this rock I will build my church" (Matt. 16:18). The rock is Peter's recognition that Jesus is the Christ, the Son of the living God. When the church is built on him and his Word, it will be a transforming church. We don't transform ourselves; he does it. The early church lived in oneness with the Spirit and prayed continually. Two thousand years later the church is often institutional rather than organic, utilitarian rather than unique, man-led rather than God-inspired. The church, as a holy creation, loses its power when it invents changes with man-made schemes rather than with prayerful dreams.

Many Christians experience pain, struggle, and grief as a result of changes in their church. Those who change churches are dubbed "church switchers," a negative title, even though a Lifeway study found that 76 percent of those who change churches are mature Christians.[1]

My husband and I are now two-time "church-switchers" due to church changes. We pray our story, at three marvelous yet imperfect churches will help church leavers navigate this painful road. We pray also that our story will give pastors and leaders "a view from the pew" that will help them minister to Christians coming and going.

# CHAPTER 1

# A FAITH JOURNEY
## "FAIREST LORD JESUS"

Faith is taking your eyes off your good self, bad self, wounded self, and looking on Jesus.

—Youth director's answering-machine message

I love the house where you live, O LORD, the place where your glory dwells.

—Psalm 26:8

**March 16, 2000**

***Main Street Church***

PASTOR EDNA THRILLS everyone—except me. As lay leader, I stifle my dubious thoughts about her theology, but they fester in my mind. Her polished biblical messages lack conviction. I don't sense the Holy Spirit. Grief over Pastor Jim's leaving could be coloring my perceptions. I sure miss him and his ministry. *Lord, help me sort this out!*

**September 24, 2007**

***Hillcrest Community Church***

The inspiring blended worship at Hillcrest Church has vanished. Loud, discordant music assaults our ears. Sets decorate the platform for each sermon series—it's similar to a stage production. The blinds are down, it's dark like a theater, and only a hymn phrase here and there is sung. Since God dwells in light and is Light, I don't understand worshipping in the dark. *Lord, help me understand. Help me worship you here!*

## MY LOSS OF FAITH AND RETURN TO FAITH

I grew up in the house of the Lord as a PK (preacher's kid). I knew and followed Jesus right from the start. I was devout in college, but became disillusioned in graduate school. Away from home and friends, I drifted away from God. I didn't find a church. I gradually severed all thoughts and ties to God and to the house of the Lord. I closed my mind to him. I didn't read anything that would remind me of him—especially not his Word. I cringed when relatives said grace before meals, and I barely tolerated an occasional church service when visiting relatives.

My spiritual life resembled a boarded-up, abandoned building; a building unsuited for me. I wanted to forget the days I lived there. I married Mike after graduate school. We had three children and enjoyed our family and our careers. Years went by. Our kids grew up.

In the late eighties, with the death of friends and a nephew, I removed a plank or two from my boarded-up heart. I began praying again. Bible verses slipped out from the cracks that were no longer boarded up. "Be still, and know that I am God" (Ps. 46:10). "My soul glorifies the Lord" (Luke 1:46). The refrain from *Godspell*, "*To see Thee more clearly, love Thee more dearly, follow Thee more nearly, day by day,*" invaded a corner of my thoughts. Glimmers of faith flickered in my mind. *We have souls; God is a loving force.*

**February 1990**

Mike and I decided to attend the charter service of a Unitarian group the first Sunday in March. We talked about finding a church. Mike said, "Let's make March church month and visit a different church each week." Mike, relaxed and easygoing, rarely took the lead in planning. I gulped at giving up my Sunday mornings for four weeks, but I thought, *Mike will never say this again.* So I agreed.

The Unitarian experience and the Episcopal one that followed it didn't impress us. The third Sunday in March we found our church home.

*Main Street Church, 1990*

We walked into Main Street United Methodist Church after decades away from God and church. I was a preacher's kid and a genuine prodigal daughter. I walked in thinking of God as a vague force and was surprised when I sensed God's presence. I choked up singing "Fairest Lord Jesus" and couldn't explain why. Mike and I wanted more people in our life. We thought we would be "casual Christians" if we could find a church we could tolerate. God had other plans.

Main Street Church was a downtown traditional church in a small town. Outwardly plain and solid, its inner beauty stunned us. The sanctuary boasted colorful stained-glass windows and one of the best organs in the region. The choir director played the organ with flair and made singing a joy. The popular forty-member choir had grown so much that it had run out of choir robes. Church membership stood at four hundred. Sunday attendance averaged two hundred.

We leaped at the chance to join the church and attended a meeting for new members six weeks after our first visit. Wesley, the pastor, taught the group about Methodists' four sources of authority: Scripture, experience, reason, and tradition, (SERT). He explained each briefly, emphasizing that Scripture is primary because it is revelation. Mike's ears perked up as we learned that we don't dispense with reason. Our faith relies on it. Wesley's emphasis on experiencing God surprised me, and pleasant memories of church from childhood and teen years flooded my mind.

Jan, the lay leader, gave us a form that said: "Main Street United Methodists are a special family. And families care and share with and for each other. Please tell us what we can do to help you feel at home." Their acceptance and desire to please us touched me. The form invited our involvement with a list of activities and needs. *We should check something*. Mike suggested we mark the adult Bible class. We weren't asked to confirm belief in the tenets of the faith. I'm not sure we could have said yes to the typical questions: "Have you asked Jesus into your heart?" "Have you accepted him as your Lord and Savior?"

The following week we attended the adult Bible class prior to the worship service. Dick, the leader, asked for prayer requests, and class members disclosed major happenings and concerns, sharing deeply with each other. For example, Dick's father-in-law was in ICU with a heart attack. In contrast, our secular friends knew little about our personal life. Dick prayed, mentioning every person or situation named. Then he taught the class giving the historical background on the book of Mark.

Sunday's worship again thrilled and uplifted us. Fourteen new members were welcomed, including us. Wesley asked the group, "As members of this congregation, will you faithfully participate in its ministries by your prayers, your presence, your gifts, and your service?"

We replied, "We will."

Wesley said to the congregation, "Members of the household of God, I commend these persons to your love and care. Do all in your power to increase their faith, confirm their hope, and perfect them in love."

Wesley's message, "Body and Soul," presented evidence that we have a soul. He mentioned near-death experiences and Ray Moody, whose book, *Life After Life*, I had read. During the service, a violist from the Richmond Symphony played "Largo" by Handel. Mike said this brought tears to his eyes. The hymn, "It Is Well with My Soul," touched me unbelievably. The organist stopped playing on the third verse, and the singers' harmony sent chills up my spine. The final verse, was loud and joyous. The combination of reverence and some informality in the service was great. I wrote in my journal, "Now I'm a Methodist and very happy about it."

My return to faith surprised me. I wished the prodigal son had a comment in the Bible about his adjustment to coming home. What a dramatic change for him and for me! My emotions rose and fell—from thrilled, joyous, and excited one minute to scared or sad the next. Sadness haunted me. I regretted the many years out of touch with God and church and I felt remorse for not teaching my children to know and love God.

We attended church and the adult Bible class weekly—in a joyful daze. We learned about the faith, met new people—as we'd hoped, and so much more. A letter to Pastor Wesley describes my transformation.

**December 16, 1990**

Dear Wesley,

One year ago I thought I was happy. But what a difference now! I've rediscovered the Bible, prayer, and worship. You helped me rediscover my soul. You put me in touch with God, Jesus, and the Holy Spirit. I woke up one morning

> singing, "I've got the joy, joy, joy, joy down in my heart." I hadn't thought of this song in years!
>
> I'm feeling, thinking, and acting differently. I'm reading the Bible and devotional literature and praying on a daily basis. I'm more giving to others and I'm more content with myself. I know I'm part of something big and I have a new family. Life has meaning and purpose. Every holiday has meaning now—especially Christmas and Easter. We'd been celebrating Xmas (with an X) for years and ignoring Easter. We're celebrating *Christ*mas this year.

As I noted in my letter to Wesley, our celebration of Christmas and Easter now recognized their holy meanings. The celebration of Advent with marvelous Christmas hymns and music by the choir touched us. Each week the choir processed into the sanctuary led by child acolytes who lit the altar candles. Each week a family lit another of the candles in the Advent wreath. At the Christmas Eve service all five candles were lit, including the center Christ candle. Similarly, preparation for Easter began with the Ash Wednesday service and the placing of ashes in the form of a cross on the forehead of believers. The ashes came from the palms waved the previous Palm Sunday. Our lives were radically changed.

## OUR FAITH GROWS

Mike had never been a church member or even a regular church attender. But God touched his mind and heart as well as mine. Childhood baggage and remorse about leaving God and church distressed me. As my trust grew, I confided in Wesley who was trained in counseling and a good listener. These sessions over several years helped me shed many past issues. Both Mike and I learned and grew spiritually throughout the 1990s. We continued in the adult Bible class and began saying grace at meals. Our worldview gradually changed.

Wesley explained the four characteristics of secular humanists:

1. The only knowledge is scientific—fact based.
2. Independence and happiness is the prime goal of life—do whatever you want.
3. Self indulgence, even narcissistic hedonism, is approved.
4. Morals are an individual or cultural choice; there are no absolutes, no right or wrong.

We certainly had been lost!

The Walk to Emmaus sparked our spiritual growth even more, and a marriage enrichment weekend enlivened our marriage. We participated in almost every activity of the church. We ran stewardship drives and served on the administrative board and other committees. Due to our expertise in mental health, we helped set up Grace Christian Counseling Center in the church in the mid-nineties. At the Center we also organized a group for couples using a national program, the Third Option.

We loved the church very much. We knew it wasn't perfect, and we knew we weren't perfect, but we were growing in our faith. We assumed others were experiencing the same strong faith and presence of Christ. And many were.

## HIJACKED BY THE HIERARCHY–APOSTASY IN THE CHURCH

In 1993 several Minnesota councils of churches, in response to the World Council of Churches Solidarity with Women agenda, organized and hosted an international conference with the purpose of "re-imagining" God, the church, and the family. The conference attacked the basic doctrines of Christianity.

The event included prayers to the goddess Sophia and a milk and honey communion-like service. Speakers denied basic Christian tenets, including the incarnation, the atonement of Jesus Christ, and the transcendence of God. A professor from Union Theological Seminary in New York told the group, "I don't think we need a theory of atonement at all ... atonement has to do so much with death ... I don't think we need folks hanging on crosses and blood dripping and weird stuff ... we just need to listen to the god within."[1] Mainline churches, including the United Methodist Church, financed and sent delegates to this event.

Shock and dismay overwhelmed Wesley and the leaders of Main Street Church when they learned about the Re-Imagining Conference. After prayer and dialog, the administrative board decided to withhold yearly apportionments, funds required by the District and the Conference. They notified our bishop to this effect.

One year later Wesley reported on a meeting with the bishop and the district superintendent, calling it "an intense conversation." The bishop admitted some unacceptable things happened at the Re-Imagining Conference and said she should have replied to our letter of last May—huge concessions for this bishop. The board voted to release the funds, relieved to have this settled.

## Change, Grief, and Reassurance

Change came in 1997 when Wesley retired after eighteen years at Main Street Church. Wesley, a wise and kindly pastor with life-changing influence on many church members, was roasted, celebrated, and many grieved his leaving. He ministered to me in the truest sense of the word—as pastor, counselor, teacher, and friend. Most significantly, he pointed me to Jesus. I grieved Wesley's leaving with many tears, not wanting to lose him as my pastor. My journal noted, "Trying to hold on to people, experiences, and the past is like trying to hold on to water."

We welcomed Jim, our new pastor, the last Sunday in June. He asked a layman to pray for him, then gave a sermon on "Remember Your First Love" from Revelation 2:1–7. He said, "I have come to comfort the afflicted and to afflict the comfortable." He received a standing ovation for an impressive message. He led a hymn of commitment at the end of the service. In my journal I predicted, "He will make us stretch and grow spiritually."

That night I dreamed God carried me down a flight of stairs and across some distance. I floated as he held me up. What a comforting dream! I thought of the verse, "Seek first his kingdom and his righteousness, and all these things will be given to you as well" (Matt. 6:33). I believed Wesley's leaving meant nothing but loss. Now I realized much would be added by knowing Jim.

Pastor Jim's personality and messages differed from Wesley's. Jim read the Bible, but had no time to read books. His messages were folksy and evangelical. Retired from the Marines as a lieutenant colonel, he had an engineering mind and was a doer. His warm personality broke both military and engineering stereotypes. Wesley crafted beautifully written sermons with references to books, scientific discoveries, and appropriate illustrations with humor. His comforting personality and messages pointed to Jesus and his love.

Jim visited every member of the church in his first three months. He started Disciple Bible Study with seventy people involved in a year-long, in-depth study. He encouraged many previously uninvolved laity to give the children's messages or lead worship. Jim served Communion at the kneeling rail (rather than passing it in the pews), and he introduced drama at Easter to convey biblical truth. He opened our downtown church for prayer at noon on Fridays and encouraged more prayer.

Jim asked me to be lay leader beginning in January 1999 as Jan wanted to step down. After praying about it, I accepted, thrilled by this opportunity to learn from and work with Jim.

Jim led groups to Promise Keepers in 1997, 1998, and then to the Promise Keepers event in Washington DC in 1999, where one million men gathered at the Washington Monument. These Promise Keeper events deeply affected Mike. In 1999 Jim led a group to Israel and Jordan, including us—the trip of a lifetime, walking where Jesus walked.

Wesley comforted us. Jim challenged us. Both modeled Jesus.

### RUMBLINGS FROM THE CONGREGATION

One year into Jim's ministry at Main Street Church, rumblings of discontent came from some back-of-the-church Christians not active in leadership, teaching, or outreach. They overtly complained about Communion—sanitary issues and not wanting to go forward. Covert issues stemmed from Jim's authority and his evangelical messages which challenged the status quo. Jim, not as diplomatic as Wesley, succeeded a beloved pastor—even Billy Graham would not have lasted very long.

In August 1999, Dick and Jan announced to the Bible class their plans to take four to six weeks off to discern God's possibly leading them to another church. What a shocking loss! The strong faith, excellent teaching, and leadership ability of both Dick and Jan would be missed. Jan regretted leaving, but followed Dick's wishes. I think Dick couldn't accept Jim's less sophisticated messages.

Despite my heavy heart, I clung to God. I cared about both Dick and Jan and had learned much from each of them. In the midst of this, I learned of other unhappy members, some of whom were close friends. Jim had given a message on Romans 12:1–8, mentioning members who are like the appendix in the body of Christ—useless. As lay leader I confronted Jim.

Although upset, Jim faced the fact some members did not hear him telling of God's love.

The following Sunday calmed my fears. Jim's message on two transfusions came from Exodus 12:1–12 about the Passover meal with blood on the doorposts. Communion followed this. Jim described Passover and Communion as the two blood transfusions. I recognized Jim's utter devotion to preaching Christ and the Bible. This touched me deeply, and I assumed it affected others also. Two months later I found out otherwise.

In late October, the personnel committee leader told me she planned to talk with our district superintendent about concerns with Jim. I couldn't convince her otherwise. In November, Jim suddenly accepted a call to his home church in Arizona—catching me and others by surprise. Pastors in the Methodist Church usually leave at the end of June. Jim gave six weeks notice and left at the end of 1999, after only two-and-a half-years at Main Street Church. His sudden leaving shocked and grieved me.

**December 31, 1999**

> Dear Father,
>
> Thank you for the many ways you have blessed us this year. Last night I wept over losing Jim and Shirley. I reread my journal and felt close to you with all the Jesus hymns playing in my head. Thank you for bringing two such special people into my life. I have learned so much from them about you, especially about giving of myself. I'm thankful I risked getting to know them. A few years ago I'm not sure I would have.

I grieved Jim's going, but remained optimistic about the new pastor to be assigned.

# CHAPTER 2

# STRANGE TEACHINGS
## "DON'T LET SATAN BLOW IT OUT!"

False teachers aren't necessarily even that obvious. They don't wear badges identifying themselves as apostates. They usually try hard not to stand out as enemies of truth. They pretend devotion to Christ and demand tolerance from Christ's followers.

—John MacArthur

If anyone teaches false doctrines and does not agree to the sound instruction of our Lord Jesus Christ and to godly teaching, he is conceited and understands nothing.

—1 Timothy 6:3–4

### MAIN STREET CHURCH, 2000

PASTOR EDNA ARRIVED at Main Street Church at the beginning of February. I met with her briefly to go over plans for Sunday. Then I boohooed about Jim leaving. Preparing a welcoming speech for her first Sunday wasn't easy, but it went okay. And Edna was great. She took off her dress shoes and put on her five hundred dollar walking shoes. (She paid four hundred dollars for an orthopedic support and one hundred dollars for the shoes.) She wore these all over Israel, walking where Jesus walked, and never wants to shake the dust off of them. "When we follow Jesus footsteps, he will go before us," she said. The Scripture described Jesus healing Peter's mother-in-law and then going alone to pray (Mark 1:29–39). "We are in ministry to heal others, and prayer must guide our decisions as a church," she proclaimed. Her ordination banner displayed the disciples' boat on the Sea of Galilee, where they dropped their nets to follow Jesus. She used this to tell about her call to the ministry and now to Main Street Church. She gave a good biblical message.

**Communion War**

The war which began when Jim initiated Communion at the kneeling rail continued with Edna. She assured me and others she wouldn't give up having people come forward for Communion. I realized later she was pressured from both sides of the issue.

Strong feelings and differing opinions about Communion were expressed in the adult Bible class. Bill claimed two rows of people didn't take Communion recently. Ronald chimed in, "I don't like Communion at the kneeling rail. It's not as personal." I said, "I think it's more personal. Maybe you mean it's not as private as taking it in the pews."

Out of the blue, Edna announced in church that Communion would not be served on the first Sunday of March and April since we would have Communion Ash Wednesday and Maundy Thursday. I called her and expressed surprise about canceling Communion. She said, "That's my prerogative." Later I wrote a letter complimenting her on her hard work and explaining my concerns:

1. Some people would not receive Communion at all during Lent because they can't come out at night.
2. We should have Communion more during Lent, not less.

Edna thanked me for the letter and admitted she hadn't thought about the people who couldn't make it in the evening. She apologized for not running the decision by me first. She had spent an hour on the phone with a seminary professor deciding what to do about Communion. He told her we were not a eucharistic church. I heard nothing about praying about her decision. To her credit she continued to serve Communion at the kneeling rail after this.

### A Lenten Class and Process Theology

Edna gave a Lenten program on Julian, a thirteenth-century contemplative.[1] In the introduction she mentioned a professor who taught process theology. I wondered, *What on earth is process theology?* Edna asked us to draw or write our description of God based on a saying from Julian, "God is all that is good." I thought, *A flower is good therefore the flower is God?* My common sense told me not to question Julian's theology (or Edna's) in the group. I drew a heart with LOVE in the middle and kept my mouth shut.

Later in an email, I asked Jim about process theology. He replied:

> Process theology teaches God is in process and always changing. God improves himself as time goes on and grows in relationship with humans. God reconfigures himself as he grasps a better understanding of people. The world is viewed as perfect and there's a subtle refuting of original sin.

Edna did a beautiful job with Holy Week services, and her messages were good, citing evidence for the resurrection as an historical fact. (Some intellectual "Christians" don't believe this, so it pleased me that she spelled it out.) A Tenebrae service (in which candles are gradually extinguished, representing the darkness of the crucifixion) ended with something new. Edna carried the last candle out of the sanctuary and we heard the door slam to represent the tomb being shut.

**Growing Concerns**

In May I met with Edna and shared my concerns about her liberal views. She acknowledged she is liberal and a process theologian. She brought up the homosexual issue and said she would not do a same-sex ceremony as long as it is against the Methodist discipline. I told her this would be my last year as lay leader.

My discontent and concerns about Edna continued. Unable to sleep, I wrote a letter to her with no intention of mailing it. As a counselor, I knew journaling would help me.

**July 10, 2000 (1:00 AM)**

Dear Edna,

I usually like, trust, and can connect with others, but not with you. In spite of attempts to reach out to you, I've been ignored, rejected, and even put down at times. I've wept buckets over this and prayed for God's help, often at my wit's end. Sunday is now the low point of my week, when for ten years it's been the high point.

You're busy, overwhelmed, or depressed all the time. This has a decidedly negative effect on me (and I assume on others). Your mood sets a negative tone at meetings. I never hear you turning to God for guidance about plans—nor do I hear you consulting with leaders in the church.

> You've taken over some areas such as the children's message. Don't you know this undermines participation by the laity? You avoid communicating with me, as lay leader. Why? I'm easy and flexible and might have some helpful ideas. It astounded me that you planned Laity Sunday. Normally, the lay leader plans this with input from the pastor and others. It's no wonder you're worn out—you try to do everything.
>
> Then there's the whole issue of your theology. Examples abound: The sermon about Jesus overriding the Ten Commandments, in which you justified abortion and stealing, appalled me. The comments about Jonah as a "wonderful parable," and your negative remark about "you knit me together in my mother's womb" (Ps. 139:13), made me question where you're leading the congregation. Process theology is another concern. I don't want to be in a church that is essentially Unitarian—or lukewarm. God led us to Main Street Church, but recently I've wondered if he wants us elsewhere. I'm angry the Methodist Church sent you, a false teacher-pastor, on the heels of an evangelical pastor. I'm sick about the change in direction of our church. No more altar calls. No more prayer at noon on Friday. No more faith in miracles.
>
> How do you see God? Obviously you don't view him as father as you never pray, "Dear Father." You said you don't like any pictures of Jesus. You're an artist. How would you paint him? Is he really your Lord and Savior?

In August the Promise Keepers group came back glowing. Edna said, "I wasn't allowed to go," and stood with her arms crossed while Glenn shared about it. During the fall, Main Street Church struggled with low attendance and finances, and the Sunday messages barely mentioned Jesus. Edna continued to compromise the gospel message, and no one held her accountable.

Edna's message about a little child leading us (Isa. 11:6) is a good example. She glorified our children who can program VCRs, think like a computer, and have lived all their lives recycling, so are aware of environmental issues. She tied this to the boy "who offered" his loaves and fish to help feed the multitudes. She said nothing about Jesus, referring vaguely to not understanding what happened there. It was a mystery. In other words, not a miracle!

### A Retreat and More Concerns

Edna planned and led a Saturday retreat at the church. In the morning we sang, did a brief Bible study, and figured out our spiritual gifts. After lunch we each listed fifteen qualities we would look for in a church if we were moving to a new community. Then we numbered them by priority. My top three core values were, "personal relationship with Jesus Christ," "biblical," and "prayer-centered seeking God's will." In groups of three we discussed our top three values and chose the group's top four values. My group merged our top three values (we were in agreement though worded differently). One person listed, "No homosexual unions." With little time, we chose this as our fourth value.

Edna had a fit when we posted this on the board. I defended our group saying this didn't mean we didn't accept homosexuals and love them. She lost her temper and yelled—out of control, saying she would not tolerate anyone not being shown love. Edna's over-the-top reaction dampened the mood of the group. She viewed anyone who differed with her as judgmental.

During a break, Kitty told me it disturbed her anyone would choose "no homosexual unions" as a core value. I explained the threat to the family in "marrying" gays and told her I thought God meant for children to have a father and a mother. She felt better after we talked, but called me on Sunday upset. Tuesday she called again, feeling better, but planned to talk to Edna. On the other side of the issue, I heard from Shirley. She had thoughts of leaving Main Street Church. Later I learned Mike listed "no gay unions" as one of his values.

I met with Edna in late October and spoke the truth. I covered every issue and even asked her if she had a personal relationship with Jesus. She replied, "Dottie, how could you ask that?" She didn't answer my question. The evidence indicated she did not know Christ. At the end of October, for example, Edna gave a children's message on how the jack-o'-lantern originated. She concluded this totally secular story with, "So don't be tricky this week."

**November 2000 E-mail to Jim**

> I'm thinking more than ever God must be calling us away from the Methodist church—it's so divided and lukewarm. I know God will guide us.

## Chapter 3

# Loss, Looking, and Leaving

## "Precious Lord, Take My Hand"

The bend in the road is not the end of the road unless you fail to make the curve.

—Anonymous

The heart of man plans his way, but the Lord establishes his steps.

—Proverbs 16:9 ESV

### Loss

IT'S DIFFICULT TO convey the angst, struggle, and pain in leaving a church so important in our lives. I put on a happy face, but began to detach from friends. Mike and I grappled with how difficult and painful leaving and finding another church would be. We agreed we'd like to be in a church with true believers; a church that was growing and alive. We prayed, "Please guide us, Lord." I wanted to run away, but couldn't.

In August 2000 I wrote in my journal:

I've been crying for two hours. I've lost so much. I've lost Jim as my pastor. His positive and upbeat attitude brought out the best in me, stretching me. I've lost the opportunity to continue to learn from him. I've lost his comfort in time of trouble. He prayed with us before my gallbladder surgery and stayed with Mike throughout it. Now I'm without a pastor. I know God is with me but …

I've lost Jim and Shirley's hugs and the many prayer times with Jim and others in the sanctuary on Fridays. I've lost meals out with Jim and Shirley, the altar calls he gave, and his messages which were challenging, practical, and often took my breath away.

I've lost a sense of the Holy Spirit in our worship and my desire to pray, because it makes me cry.

I've lost a church that was coming alive.

I've lost some self-esteem in all this. I don't feel loving or connected, I want to withdraw. I don't fit in with Edna's ministry and with Main Street Church now, but we're so involved here. How can this work out positively?

I've lost my ability to be open with others, because it could divide the church.

I've lost my peace of mind, and I've hurt Mike's peace of mind with all this turmoil.

I've lost acceptance and love for others because I feel very critical and untrusting of Edna.

I've lost a biblically true pastor who was leading our church to the truth.

Lord, I need your help and deliverance from this overwhelming pain. I give all these losses to you. Help me trust you. My future is in your hands. I know in my head you're in control.

I coped with my pain by seeking help outside Main Street Church in a number of ways. The e-mail contacts with Jim gave me a place to share our struggles. He knew us, knew the church, and knew about process theology. He was my sounding board.

Mike and I participated in the Emmaus community, a source of very inspiring worship once a month. We both served on Emmaus teams in 2000 and 2001. This involved weekly preparation meetings for six weeks followed by a weekend with new "pilgrims." These meetings filled the gap for us spiritually.

In the spring of 2000, I joined an ecumenical, charismatic prayer group held weekly during the day at a local Presbyterian church. I confided my concerns to them and asked for prayers. The support from this group helped immensely and taught me much. I met true believers and valiant prayer warriors there. The group deepened my prayer life and helped me focus on Christ and his promises.

I struggled at the prayer meetings. I wanted to run away from Main Street Church. The group said, "Don't you dare leave unless God tells you to." I agreed with this theology until a friend suggested we should "flee false teaching." After a Bible search of every reference to false teaching, I came to the conclusion these Scriptures were God's permission, or even his guidance, telling us to leave Main Street Church.

Discontentment gripped me. Edna's false teaching and character issues cast a dark shadow over Main Street Church and over my soul. At home I cried, prayed, and struggled. Mike and I wrestled with what to do. It didn't seem right to leave the church until I completed my term as lay leader at the end of 2000. Mike was adamant we couldn't leave even then due to our responsibilities with the counseling center. Conflict between us simmered until we finally talked it out. We hadn't seen the obvious—the counseling center, incorporated separately, had board members from other churches. We could continue in leadership there after leaving the church.

On January 1, I was free at last—no longer the lay leader. What a relief! My concerns about Edna had not changed.

I expected her Christmas messages to be biblical and inspirational. They were not. I noticed her calls to worship and benedictions seemed strange, and on Christmas Eve I realized why. She used the phrase, "as we have been liberated." I recalled Wesley talking about liberation theology and its connection with Marxism and the feminist movement. I looked up liberation theology and feminist theology on the Internet, and they are both tied in to process theology.

**January 1, 2001**

> Dear Father,
>
> Thank you for guiding us through the year 2000. The last few months were intensely painful, as you know. We've decided to "flee false teaching" as your word advises—leaving Main Street Church. Help us stay strong in our faith and in our love for each other. The issues have put us to the test. Help us discern where you're leading us. As we take steps to leave Main Street Church, help us do so with love and grace. It will be difficult for many who care about us—as well as for us.

### LOOKING

We searched for another church, spacing out our absences so they wouldn't be obvious. Mike agreed to go elsewhere at least once a month. Visiting other churches lifted a weight from my shoulders and fed my need for worship. The adventure and newness of each church energized me. We discovered that every church has its own culture, traditions, and ambiance.

Fifth Street Baptist Church welcomed us, had a huge choir (though not as good as Main Street's), and the minister gave a very biblical sermon. But we didn't sense much energy.

Our friends, Joe and Pat, lost their youngest son. His memorial service at the Vineyard touched and impressed us, and the pastor gave a memorable message. Later we returned to a worship service at the Vineyard. Pastor Len gave an impressive message—but I missed the organ and hymns. We attended the Vineyard a third time, enthused about Pastor Len's thoughtful and biblical messages. Mike didn't think we fit in there, and I could see why. The majority of the congregation was under forty.

We went to Hilltop Baptist Church and enjoyed it—but liked the Vineyard pastor better. One Sunday I visited Eastside Methodist Church with my friend Kristen. Mike had a cold and stayed home. Eastside's pledges had increased 80 percent the previous year, and many new people had joined this church. We sang great hymns, a few Emmaus choruses, and heard a biblical message. The words to songs were displayed on a screen up front, and the bulletin included an outline of the sermon, both new to us.

On Easter and again on Mother's Day we visited a church in the city with Steve, Ellen, and Susan, our son, daughter-in-law and daughter—and we loved it, though it was a forty-minute drive. We were attracted by Hillcrest Church's friendly congregation, blended and traditional services, many children, adults of all ages, and good messages by a younger pastor. We realized that going there would make it easier for Main Street Church to accept our leaving. We could say we wanted to worship with our family. We decided to try it during the summer.

## LEAVING

On our last Sunday at Main Street Church, God confirmed our leaving, announcing it as obviously as a flashing billboard. The sermon titled "Endings and Beginnings" (amazing!) was given by Larry, pastor/counselor from the counseling center. Larry talked of graduations, deaths, and other transitions, tying this into Genesis 2, Revelation 22:1–5, and John 17:1–5. We need to look way back and see God is in charge, and look ahead to the promise of Revelation, but live for today.

We told the Bible class our plan (God's really) to go to church with our son and his family during the summer. Our new beginnings seemed full of promise. God's confirmation of his plan filled me with awe. I wrote in my journal, "Thank you, Lord. Forgive my doubting and struggling and 'Lead me on, precious, Lord.'"

## Chapter 4

# A Big Surprise Church
## "Where He Leads Me, I Will Follow"

Loving God Profoundly—Loving People Passionately
—Hillcrest Church letterhead

If I speak in the tongues of men and of angels, but have not love, I am only a resounding gong or a clanging cymbal.
—1 Corinthians 13:1

DURING THE SUMMER of 2001 we attended Hillcrest Community Baptist Church, worshipping with our son and daughter-in law, and we joined an adult Bible class. In 2003, after selling our home, we moved close to the church and our children.

The American Baptist Church's commitment to the Bible as their final authority inspired our trust. They don't subscribe to any creed. Local autonomy rules, with no hierarchy. Each local congregation governs itself with every member having an equal vote. The American Baptist web page states, "We believe in the right of every congregation to exercise authority under God for its own life and ministry. We also believe in the right of every congregation to choose voluntarily whether or not to associate with other congregations."[1] We knew the pastor would stay a good long time and the congregation would select the next pastor. No "eminent domain" changes, no false teachers, only transformation, we thought.

Hillcrest Community Church was founded in 1942 in a residential area of the city. In 1980 they moved to their present location in a growing suburban area. To accommodate growth they added an activities center and a preschool wing in 1995, and a new sanctuary and Christian education wing in 1998. When we arrived, membership was 1,800, and they held a Saturday night service and two Sunday morning services.

The sanctuary of Hillcrest Church captivated us with its light and airy appearance. A wall of windows along two sides brought in natural light. A Communion table with flowers and candles graced the area in front of the platform. A large cross and a window above the baptistery added to the beauty and holiness of the sanctuary.

We gradually connected with others, remembered names, and learned the new church culture. This large, affluent church refreshed and excited us. Meeting many new people all at once plopped us into a captivating adventure. The Bible class welcomed us with open arms. Six members, all as knowledgeable as Dick and Jan, took turns teaching. The class didn't go off on tangents or play "ain't it awful," and we applied the text to our lives. (What a novel idea!)

We loved Hillcrest Church, noticing only positives and unaware of any negatives. We enjoyed meeting new people and worshipping in a less traditional way with a younger congregation. Discovering new biblical insights from the sermons and the Bible classes stimulated us.

Pastor Ted's first message after a summer sabbatical urged us to keep growing. Ted asked, "Are you willing to move to the next level in your relationship with God?" He suggested we close our eyes during Communion, enhancing the prayerfulness of it. This touched me deeply.

In the fall we discovered from Hillcrest's web page that the church originated in Linden in 1942 and moved in 1980, changing its name. We were married in Linden Community Baptist Church! Awe and wonder filled me—seeing God's plan so carefully and completely arranged. He led us to the church where we were married, and to my Dad's denomination. Steve and his family attended here and Susan, our daughter, lived across the street. Only God could have arranged all this!

Pastor Ted arrived at Hillcrest in the mid-nineties. He passionately promoted his vision to reach seekers, unbelievers, and young families. Ted, in his mid-forties, was an excellent speaker. His demeanor toward us was cordial, but not warm. Before joining the church, we met with Ted to get acquainted and to have our questions answered. We also attended a reception for new members at his home. On Sundays Ted mingled in the welcome center between services. Initially, he shook hands with everyone at the end of each service, but discontinued this when the church went to three morning services.

We joined the class for new members, meeting six Sunday nights for dinner, teaching, and discussion. We were divided into groups and given a notebook with information and blanks to fill in. The teaching described Hillcrest's beliefs about God, Jesus, the church, baptism, the Holy Spirit, the Lordship of Christ, and the church's organizational structure and mission.

The teaching, well presented by several of the pastors, edified and enlightened us. We enjoyed the people in our group. Due to the large membership, these connections didn't continue except with our deacon group leaders. Hillcrest Church required three things of new members—confession of faith in Jesus Christ, attendance at the membership class with each person giving their testimony in the small groups, and baptism.

Though happy here, we missed Main Street Church as described in my prayer journal.

## PRAYER OF AMBIVALENCE

**October 2001**

Dear Lord,

Thank you for guiding us to Hillcrest Church. Your fingerprints are all over our coming here. It's way outside the box of our thinking. In spite of this and the awesome spiritual level of the church, I'm unsettled, uncertain, and even depressed about leaving Main Street Church. Forgive my lack of faith, but this is a huge change.

I miss the personal contact with a minister. I know I need to trust you. I'm spiritually stronger now and need to depend on you, not a pastor. I'm excited about the opportunities for spiritual growth at Hillcrest. The Bible class is excellent, and many new people are coming into our lives here. Keep us in your care, and keep us hungering for you and growing.

## BAPTISM

At the new member class, Pastor Ted gave an inspiring talk about the scriptural basis for baptism by immersion. His baptism at age twelve didn't mean much to him, so he chose to be baptized again as a young adult. After hearing his story, and praying about it, I decided to be baptized again. Mike and I talked about this, and he chose to be baptized also. This thrilled me because Mike had no baptismal record. He assumed he was baptized as an infant, but his mother died when he was five. Choosing baptism signaled a new surrender step for both of us. My Baptist upbringing pictured baptism as a symbolic act of dying to self, being buried in the water, and then resurrected to new life in Christ. Jesus modeled it and commanded it.

We were baptized on October 28, 2001. Steve and Ellen joined the church at the same time on confession of faith. The baptism service resembled my father's. Ted asked if we accepted Jesus as our Lord and Savior. We replied "Yes," and as we were immersed, he said, "I baptize you in the name of the Father and the Son and the Holy Spirit." Ted commented to Mike, "This was a big step for you." Fifty-nine people joined the church and nineteen were baptized. The welcome at the front of the church after the service made it official, and many people greeted us. What a special day!

## Nostalgia for Main Street Church

Our longing for Main Street Church continued even though we enjoyed the new connections and the inspiring worship at Hillcrest Church. Changing churches is like trying to choose a new spouse before the divorce is final. We had our foot in the door of both churches for quite a while. Ambivalence stalked us. Thrilled with life in our new church one day, gave way to doubts and longings the next day. Two journal illustrations of this follow.

**January 2002**

> We're enjoying our new church, but we miss Main Street Church—the hymns, the organ, and the kneeling rail. Changing churches is hard. We're active at Hillcrest on Sundays and at Main Street during the week. We're in the *Disciple Bible* class at Main Street Church and still helping at Grace Counseling Center, so it's a bit strange.

**October 2003**

We attended the funeral of a friend, Roxie, from Main Street Church. I felt a mixture of emotions. Pastor Edna officiated, adding to my confusion and sorrow. I recalled my prior closeness to Main Street Church members and felt sad. I want to put the past behind me, but I long for those days.

## HIGH NOTES AT HILLCREST

In November of 2001, Pastor Ted gave a brilliant message titled, "Do All Roads Lead to God?" He spelled out the fact that Jesus is the only way to God. He detailed the basic teachings of other faiths and said Christianity is the only faith in which God comes to us—in which God is personal and sends his Son to die for us. This remarkable message received a standing ovation.

In November, 2002, in connection with a sermon series on "Thanks Living," Hillcrest Church gave out a flyer recommending members increase their giving 1 percent a year. In Ted's message he said a tithe is the level where giving should begin. "People ask, 'Can I graduate up to this increase each year.' If you want to continue to rob God, you can graduate slowly," he said, referring to Malachi 3:8. This surprised me since the flyer suggested a gradual increase. It also convinced me of the unity and devoutness of the Hillcrest members. It thrilled me to be in a church with no financial struggles and with generous giving to missions and outreach—18 percent of their budget.

In the following journal entry, I note my spiritual growth at Hillcrest.

**March 2004**

The Sunday Bible class takes my breath away and causes me to ponder God's Word. The ladies' weekday Bible studies have moved me back on track spiritually, especially *Listening Prayer* and *Who I Am in Christ.* These studies have been life-changing. I'm trusting and obeying God more. I'm facing my sin and realizing how much I sit on his throne wanting to be god, wanting to be in control. God nudged me to join the prayer team. I'm praying for people after worship, and this is stretching me.

## Active Members

We were active members of Hillcrest Church. In addition to Bible class and church on Sundays, we participated in marriage retreats and men's or women's retreats. I attended ladies' Bible studies every year. Mike assisted a Sunday school class for four-year-olds and joined a golf group. I joined the prayer team and attended prayer meetings. We helped on a planning team for a 2004 and 2005 spiritual retreat. In 2005 we joined the Alpha class at Hillcrest, and a small group evolved from this.

Hillcrest Church is noted for its outreach to the community. Mike helped in the used-book ministry driving long distances to collect used Christian books for missionaries. We both volunteered when the church held outreaches in the surrounding community. Mike helped monthly, and I occasionally, at a local clothing ministry.

We brought the Third Option, a ministry to hurting couples, to Hillcrest Church, organizing and leading this weekly year-round group for five years. This program required a large staff of couples, some to teach and facilitate, and some, who had resolved major problems, to tell their stories. The staff of this group became a special group of friends. The years leading the Third Option enriched our life and our marriage.

Though I missed a close tie to a pastor, God provided two women as mentors and friends. Lynn, a Spirit-filled, knowledgeable, and affirming teacher, led the spiritual retreats we helped with and taught most of the ladies' Bible studies I attended. Madison, a lively, engaging woman with many gifts, led our small group and continues to lead it today. Madison also is my prayer partner.

We had found our church and were at home there ... until....

## Chapter 5

# Too Many Spectacular Changes

## "I Need Thee Every Hour"

A pastor shouldn't change or move anything until he knows who it belongs to and how long it's been there, even if it's a dead dog under the front pew.

—A Methodist pastor in the 1990s

I will refresh the weary and satisfy the faint.

—Jeremiah 31:25

IN A FOUR-year span, we experienced a dozen major changes at Hillcrest Church. Some changes were a normal part of life—a minister retired, a friend died. We could understand, grieve, and accept these changes. Other changes were difficult—more like eminent domain, a total upheaval of a neighborhood (a church) by authorities. Count the changes we endured at Hillcrest.

### Change in Worship Times

Hillcrest Church announced plans for three services on Sunday mornings. Instead of services at nine and eleven o'clock, we would worship at eight-thirty, ten, and eleven-thirty. This was a significant change for the entire church. It affected Sunday volunteer jobs as well as worship and classes.

## Class Changes

Our large 9:00 AM class met with Pastor Ted to clarify the changes in times of worship. We were told our class would meet at 8:30 AM, and the class needed to split. After some griping, grieving, and struggling by class members, the class did split. About half of the class members decided to meet at 10:00 AM and one member, a pastor in a parachurch organization, announced he would teach the class. We remained in the 8:30 class since we attended the ten o'clock worship service with our son and daughter-in-law. We missed the friends who split to go to the ten o'clock class.

## Staff and Friends Leave with Secrecy

*Kathleen*, associate pastor and a lovely person, resigned. She gave beautiful messages, solemnized the Maundy Thursday service every Easter, led women's ministries, and excelled at every task of the senior pastor. She left due to depression, taking a leave of absence, and later resigning. Something at church triggered her depression. Secrecy surrounded this.

*Marla*, a warm, gifted woman, in charge of worship arts and deeply involved in the life of the church, also left. This enabled the church to go high tech. I wondered, *Was she forced out?*

*Beth*, a prayer-team leader, disappeared from church—no longer on the team. No one would answer my questions—secrecy again.

*Josh*, involved in prayer ministry and Alpha, disappeared from church with secrecy.

I wrote in my journal:

**June 2006**

> Sadness and tears this morning cleansed my soul—though I'm not sure what prompted my outburst. I thought about Beth and Kathleen and Marla—missing them and wishing I knew why they left.

## More Losses

*Devin*, the Music Minister and Care Pastor, a very caring person, was the third staff member who left. He led classical music performances like "Elijah," with a large orchestra and choir. He filled two jobs, and it took a number of people to replace him! He left to retire, but must have been exhausted.

*Will,* a warm, friendly man from our adult Bible class, died from a chronic illness. The entire church grieved his death. It was Will who introduced himself and invited us to his Sunday-school class when we first came. Though not the leader or a teacher of the class, Will was the heart of the class and a dynamic influence throughout the church. The class continued, but Will's absence changed the group.

## High Tech Changes

*Blaine*, the new worship pastor, was young, dynamic, and devout. With his arrival the church switched to all contemporary music (except for the traditional service). The church went high tech, installing screens on both sides of the sanctuary, and hiring new staff to produce videos to accompany the pastor's messages.

*The children's ministry* also went high tech and glitzy with energetic leaders, a gym redecorated with loud-patterned carpet and video games (and no more basketball available).

The halls around the children's Sunday-school rooms and the rooms themselves were painted with pictures appealing to children. Later, three large screens and more video-game machines were installed in the large room where the youth met.

## CHURCH NAME CHANGE

The church dropped the word "Baptist" from the church name becoming simply Hillcrest Community Church. Intense meetings about the name change occurred with the vote postponed once for a prolonged period. Church leaders said the official name would include Baptist and we would remain part of the denomination. The letterhead and church signs would read Hillcrest Community Church. The reasons:

1. Unchurched people, turned off by the Baptist label, won't even come into the building.
2. According to studies on church growth, churches attract more members when the denomination name is dropped.

When the name change took effect, some members left Hillcrest. Some who stayed remained disturbed about it several years later.

## CHANGES IN WORSHIP

The worship service changed dramatically. Contemporary music prevailed, rather than the previous blend of hymns and contemporary songs. Loud, discordant music hurt ears, jarred nerves, and sounded as appealing as chalk on a blackboard. As described in chapter 1, we had "sets" for each sermon series, with the blinds down making it dark like a movie theatre. Many grumbled about the changes, and not just the over-fifty crowd.

## My Angst Continues

Here are journal entries expressing my frustration and confusion.

**October 2006**

> Things confused me in church yesterday. The music began with a discordant, loud number, not musical. I wanted to put my hands over my ears. I longed for a quiet, holy sanctuary with heavenly organ music and uplifting hymns. Lord, why the changes in worship? I'm praying for Blaine and the leadership to come to their senses. Help them see what enhances worship and what detracts from it.

**December 11, 2006**

> The Christmas musical with four identical services was a performance rather than a worship service in my mind. "Lord, do you want all the high tech stuff, the spotlights and videos? Does this reach younger people? Do they sense your presence and learn of you in the loud music and glaring lights? Let your still, small voice be heard."

**December 18, 2006**

> Yesterday's worship upset me, and I woke up in turmoil about Hillcrest Church. Still no Christmas carols, no silence, no marvelous Christmas classical music or beautiful solos. I cried and felt confusion about this.

### January 8, 2007

> I'm sad and tearful about Hillcrest music and my thwarted desire to worship with others in a deep, meaningful way, to worship as a church. I wondered if I should contact church leaders. Madison's reaction was neutral. "Well, I'm already half deaf." Lynn suggested I say it in a loving way—such as, "It's a health issue," and call the chairman of the deacon board. I have other things to do and would rather not focus on this.
>
> When I talked with Mike, he suggested we go to the early service, but he seemed annoyed—which annoyed me, so I dropped it. I'm so sad that many in churches today are not learning the great classic hymns with profound lessons in theology in every verse. Nor are they learning or hearing the great classical music—or even the more recent Gaither hymns. Music touches my soul—now my Sundays are robbed of this experience. I don't understand why we need all the technology. Why can't we open the blinds and enjoy God's light and see the cross? I miss the pastoral prayer, the quiet, serene atmosphere of Main Street Church, the complete Communion—with all the Scripture and with each person coming forward and kneeling to receive it. Yet there are more members at Hillcrest who truly know you, and many opportunities to learn here. *Lord, help me sort all this out.*

I lamented the worship changes often. We never dreamed we would leave this church, but now we were contemplating it.

## MARITAL DIFFERENCES

In April 2007 I fell back into the pit again. When I criticized a worship service with the children singing for a full half hour, Mike suggested, with sarcasm in his voice, that we look for another church. As a result I sulked all day. The process of change had me at my wit's end. I prayed, "*Lord, help us resolve our differences about church and know where you want us.*"

After many long talks, we decided to attend the traditional service hoping this would meet our worship needs. It didn't. This service, with organ, hymns, Scripture, and prayers, puzzled us even more—it lacked something. Attendance of three hundred in a sanctuary that held eight hundred didn't help any.

## Sadness Continues

Confusion and sadness about worship continued throughout 2007.

**November 2007**

> The singing policeman's patriotic music and testimony were excellent, but the worship morphed into entertainment, with little congregational singing, and a bright light shining in my eyes. Ted's sermon, "Can You Afford It?", didn't fit with the rest of the service. My comments are petty when I focus on God and his grand scheme of things.

**December 24, 2007**

> Ted gave a wonderful Christmas Eve message: "Christmas—Presents or Presence." Mike viewed this service as I did—excellent message, terrible music with loud drums. "Lord, guide us where we can worship you and grow."

## Searching for a Supplemental Church

In my reading I discovered the idea of attending two churches. We decided to look for a supplemental church for occasional hymns, prayers, and quiet, meaningful worship—but continue as members at Hillcrest Church. We launched our search on

December 30, 2007, a day when Hillcrest virtually did away with worship, passing out a CD for family worship at home. Hillcrest held one small worship service in the chapel. We visited Christ United Methodist Church that day and enjoyed their traditional worship in spite of low attendance and a guest speaker. I wrote in my journal: "I'm very uncertain about this venture, but Mike seems interested in exploring other churches. *Lord, guide us in this.*"

"*Lord, guide us.*" My prayer repeated over and over. "*Lord, guide us.*"

# Chapter 6

# Struggling, Searching, and Leaving

## "We'll Understand It Better By and By"

> What the church needs most desperately is holy fear. The passion to please God more than the culture and community in which we spend these few, short years.
>
> —Chuck Colson

> The very steps we take come from God; otherwise how would we know where we're going?
>
> —Proverbs 20:24 (The Message)

### Struggling

**January 2008**

MY DEPRESSION, ANGER, and self-pity due to repeated disappointment with Hillcrest worship continued into the New Year. Sadness about the world's rejection of God and the decline of the church gripped me. Reading *Soul Tsunami* by Leonard Sweet, a book about the postmodern church, didn't help. I prayed, "Lord, guide us as we search. Help Mike and me discern your will and grow in the process. I pray my unrest leads us to a church with deeper worship of you. I feel lost Lord. Help me be lost in you."

A quiet, cold weekend at home allowed time to draft an e-mail to the deacon chairman about my discontent with Hillcrest Church. Mike read my letter and became grim and negative, depressing me more. Later I reminded Mike that God moved us from Main Street Church and used us at Hillcrest. God would guide us now. Mike admitted he doesn't like the "sets" or the applause (as for a performance) during worship. I sent the e-mail.

## January 28, 2008

Dear Brandon,

I'm writing regarding the many changes in worship this past year. I have prayed and struggled about these issues. I know the leadership hears many complaints and strives to satisfy varying tastes and viewpoints. You have a tough job. But you need to know members' thoughts, struggles, and needs.

My husband and I joined Hillcrest Church in the fall of 2001, after attending for six months. We have attended the 10:00 AM worship almost exclusively because our son and daughter-in-law prefer this service and we enjoy worshipping with them. The blended ten o'clock worship attracted us, in part, to Hillcrest Church. The changes since have been major. The changes detract from worship and leave me depressed instead of filled with the Holy Spirit. Here's a list of concerns:

- The music is so loud it hurts ears and is difficult to sing. The drummer drowns out the voices, and the words are repetitious, leaving the congregation uninvolved in worship.
- We sing only occasional lines of hymns. We're losing the great theology in hymns. Some of the hymns need updating, but some are fine as they are. How can anyone improve on "How Great Thou Art?" Why not quietly

sing worshipful choruses? Many of these are sung on the Walk to Emmaus or by Gaither.

- Why no Christmas carols? Even seekers know and crave these. Our daughter, a non-believer, commented on this negatively.
- Another major change is the use of sets for each sermon series. The time, work, and money put into these makes no sense. The sanctuary is beautiful without them, and with them, it looks like a theater. Are we there to be entertained?
- The bright spotlights are disturbing.
- The dark sanctuary dampens the mood of worship. It's so dark, it's difficult to find the pew rack for Communion cups. Jesus is the Light of the world. Why are we worshipping him in the dark?
- The Maundy Thursday service was special, and it's gone. Cross Walk took its place and drew many families for a hands-on experience that touched and taught people, young and old alike. There were long lines waiting to get in. But it's also gone. Why?
- Good worship can take many forms and leads to spiritual growth, but should involve everyone. Some of the most traditional and singable music is used during the offering without including the congregation. Couldn't we sing along? We need to be involved, not entertained.

This summarizes the issues as I see them. There is so much positive happening at Hillcrest Church, but worship is a crucial function of a church and a need in all hearts. We need to be filled with the Holy Spirit in order to go out into the mission-field and effectively share the love of Christ. We don't plan to leave Hillcrest, though we plan to look for a place to go on Maundy Thursday and other holidays to supplement our involvement here.

In Christ's love,
Dottie Parish

I sent my letter by e-mail with no request for a receipt and no copy to the pastor or others. I received no reply. A year later, Brandon learned about my e-mail and contacted me. He missed it because he was out of the country when I sent it. He had hundreds of emails to go through when he returned. He apologized and addressed my issues verbally.

### SEARCHING

On January 13 we attended two churches because the timing of the services made this possible. We discovered Grace Bible Church through their informative website. Grace Church surprised Mike and me. They greeted us warmly, and the service touched us. I loved the focus on God and his Word with no attempt to entertain or win seekers. Reservations popped up in my mind. *Would I like spending a year hearing messages only from Isaiah, as they have done?*

We returned to Christ Church—a church we had visited at the end of the year. This very liturgical Methodist church delighted us. The choir in robes processed in and out accompanied by organ music. We relished the relaxed and reverent Communion service with Scripture, careful explanation, and worshipers coming forward to receive it. On the negative side, terrible acoustics diminished the singing. The pastor's message and delivery neither inspired nor impressed us, and no one engaged us except for a few feeble handshakes.

Early in February we worshiped at King's United Methodist Church some distance from our home. It reminded us of Main Street Church. Their beautiful colonial sanctuary—like a Kinkade painting—brimmed with openness and light. We used hymn books—they had no screens! We delighted in the organ music, wonderful hymns, and large traditional choir. The service included many prayers, time for confession, and an explanation of the need for confession. The pastor showed warmth and gave a biblical message.

We returned a few days later for their Ash Wednesday service, and Ellen, our daughter-in-law, went with us. We sang six verses of "Just as I Am" and "There is a Fountain Filled with Blood." The hymns, responsive readings, time of confession, and the pastor's message touched and filled us. We received ashes on our foreheads and Communion. We wished this church was closer.

The following Sunday at Montrose United Methodist Church, a name tag attached to the front of each bulletin gave instructions for use. We dutifully wrote our names and put them on. Then we noticed no one else had done so. We took ours off. This attempt to be welcoming and friendly failed because the congregation didn't follow through.

We did enjoy the small choir, children's message, hymns, responsive reading, Apostles' Creed, and pastoral prayer with the Lord's Prayer. The message lasted a brief fifteen minutes. Mike noted their quiet, reflective service differed from worship at Hillcrest.

## More Struggling

### Glamour and Glitz and Bending the Truth

One Sunday in February 2008, Kay, a twenty-year-old singer and member of Hillcrest Church, led the worship. Pastor Ted instructed us *not* to sing along with her. We sat in the dark the entire hour. Ted touted his vision for Hillcrest Church as a center for healing (Celebrate Recovery, Grief Share) and as a platform for young artists. Kay gave one brief prayer and Ted led a brief time of silent prayer at the end.

Ted's message, the first of a series on prayer, featured the account of Jesus upsetting the money changers. Jesus said, "My house will be called a house of prayer, but you are making it a 'den of robbers'" (Matt. 21:13). According to Ted, the money changers were "exploiting the poor, the sick, and the weak, and we need to welcome these—not be self-centered as are those who complain about the sanctuary being too dark/too light, the music too loud/too soft."

Ted's message distorted the meaning of Jesus' words. The bargaining and swindling by the money changers and the temple authorities kept the pilgrims from encountering God and interfered with an atmosphere of worship. Instead of teaching about the context and meaning of the Scripture, Ted used his message to criticize those who complained about the music.

My criticisms about this service frustrated Mike. Ellen agreed with me and wanted to look elsewhere, but couldn't due to Steve and their children.

## MORE SEARCHING

We visited Bethesda United Methodist Church—the friendliest church we'd seen, but it didn't seem like the "right" place for us. Mike didn't want to look at other churches after this, preferring to stay at Hillcrest Church. Our plan had unraveled. Mike and I no longer agreed about searching. Frustration and depression overwhelmed me.

At our small group, Madison and Buzz asked what church we went to on Sunday. I answered, but said no more. I thought if we discussed this in the group, my negative impressions of Hillcrest Church could be a hindrance to others.

On Palm Sunday Mike relented, and we returned to Grace Church. The service lifted my spirit, taught and thrilled me, and made me conclude we had found our supplemental church. I sensed God's Spirit at Grace Church and exulted in no glitz, no bright lights, no big promotional campaigns, no clapping in the service. The Palm Sunday message was tied to the purpose of Jesus being here. The pastor said Jesus described his Kingdom in the Sermon on the Mount (Matt. 5–7), and then he demonstrated it in Matthew 8 by healing a leper, a gentile, and a woman—three people who were lowly, looked down on, or avoided. The reverent service included singable music, a baby dedication, and a mission moment. And a friend from Bible Study Fellowship greeted Mike.

After the service at Grace Church, Mike went to Hillcrest to help with the class of four-year-olds and I met Ellen and Lydia (my daughter-in-law and granddaughter) at Covenant United Methodist Church. Their traditional Palm Sunday service included children marching in waving palms, and the congregation waving them at the end. Two services on Palm Sunday delivered manna to my soul.

## More Struggling

### Holy Thursday Past

At Main Street Church and Hillcrest Church, the Maundy Thursday service during Holy Week was a very reverent Communion service. The service remembered the last Passover supper Jesus held with his disciples the night before his crucifixion. Kathleen, our associate pastor, led Hillcrest's Maundy Thursday services until she left.

A new and creative Easter event called Cross Walk followed. The Hillcrest welcome center was transformed into a garden, and the sanctuary featured stations around the perimeter. We removed our shoes at the sanctuary entrance to symbolize being on holy ground. Children participated with parents in stations representing the events of the week and the meaning of Christ's death on the cross. This event inspired and taught many. Cross Walk had disappeared in recent years to make way for the Easter musical performed all weekend.

**Holy Thursday 2008**

It surprised us to learn about a Maundy Thursday service at Hillcrest led by Sean and Barb's small group. This was held in the chapel at Hillcrest, a room designed to hold seventy-five people, maximum. Mike and I attended the service and found it packed with at least a hundred people. The large turnout, marvelous hymns, and quiet worship touched my soul. Barb gave a thought-provoking talk about the Seder Passover meal, tying it in to Maundy Thursday, and then we had a reflective Communion.

**Easter 2008**

The Easter service at Hillcrest Church greatly distressed me. There were no traditional Easter hymns, only a contemporary version of Amazing Grace—with the blinds down, bright lights on the platform, setting of a garden, and the praise team "entertaining" us much of the time. And Ted's "Resurrection" message gave no account of the first Easter morning. Ted wasn't a false teacher, but he certainly adapted the message to the culture and did so on the most holy day of the faith. *Lord, are you guiding us to leave Hillcrest? Thank you for conquering death and for the hope that Easter gives us.*

**Hillcrest Prayer Meeting—April 2008**

The first prayer meeting held in the sanctuary included silence and encouragement to move around, kneel, or come to the mike. Pastor Ted spoke briefly about evangelism rather than prayer! He read about Christ's ascension. Two angels said to the disciples, "Why do you stand here looking into the sky?" (Acts 1:11). Ted's version, "Why do you stand here with your hands in your pockets? Go into all the world as my witnesses." He left out the fact that after Christ's ascension the disciples were "constantly in prayer" (v. 14) until the day of Pentecost *forty days later*. Ted seems to be bending Scripture to get the message he wants to give—and his message is always "go and do," even in a prayer meeting.

## LEAVING

We left Hillcrest Church without saying good-bye. We handled our leaving with more closure when we left Main Street Church, announcing it to our class and to close friends. The largeness of Hillcrest Church made our connections to many friends tenuous. We had retired from the weekly marriage group in 2007, distancing us from the members and the sixteen Third Option staff. We no longer attended our Sunday-school class, so we didn't even say good-bye to them. We didn't know where we were going, so it was easier to say nothing.

We left because I could no longer stay at Hillcrest Church. For a year and a half I prayed and struggled trying to worship in spite of the loud music, flashing lights, and passive entertainment. Without meaningful worship, my soul wilted like a flower with no water. My legitimate needs were not being met. *God must want us elsewhere*, I believed. Our plan to find a supplemental church changed to finding a church. Mike heard, understood, and accepted this. God was faithful and helped us grow through the struggles. God took us to our new church. But for a while I was in church limbo.

## CHURCH LIMBO

Dear Father,

I'm in church limbo, a place of oblivion, a forlorn and forgotten area. Church limbo is painful. Without a church, I feel lost, like an abandoned child, alone. Your Word reminds me, "'I know the plans I have for you,' declares the LORD, 'plans to prosper you and not to harm you, plans to give you hope and a future'" (Jer. 29:11). Lord, guide us in discovering your plan.

# Chapter 7

# A Smaller Church, Big Surprise

## "The Church's One Foundation"

When the Church is absolutely different from the world, she invariably attracts it. It is then that the world is made to listen to her message, though it may hate it at first.

—D. Lloyd-Jones

You also, like living stones, are being built into a spiritual house to be a holy priesthood, offering spiritual sacrifices acceptable to God through Jesus Christ.

—1 Peter 2:5

GRACE BIBLE CHURCH, located only blocks from Hillcrest Church, is an independent, elder-led church. Founded in 1962, the church built a new building in 1985 at the present location. A 2003 expansion doubled the size of the building. Pastor Paul, called to Grace Church in 1998, speaks with eloquence and possesses an amazing grasp of Scripture. His messages give verse-by-verse lessons through an entire book of the Bible.

The Grace Church building, a modern one-story structure, features a spacious welcoming area with expansive windows.

The five-hundred-seat sanctuary has a light and airy appearance due to a skylight in the vaulted ceiling and indirect perimeter lighting.

Grace Church attracted us each time we came. I liked their leisurely schedule with two identical worship services, an hour and fifteen minutes long, with Sunday-school classes concurrently and a half-hour in between. This schedule helped me quiet myself and meet God. Nothing seemed rushed. Simple things such as the call to worship and the benediction became manna to this starving pilgrim.

Though Grace Church attracted us, Mike and I also experienced a great deal of ambivalence about it. We went through cycles of fascinating discovery and learning followed by doubt and ambivalence.

## Discovery

One Sunday in April, we connected with Pastor Paul and a few of the members. Paul's message from Isaiah 51 on God's righteousness and his extensive grasp of the Bible awed us. On the way home Mike commented, "They couldn't be more accepting of us." I agreed. Relief and amazement at finding Grace Church overwhelmed me that afternoon and tears of joy flowed. Then ambivalence and doubt returned. *This is such a big change.*

Another Sunday I had little anticipation because I knew Paul wouldn't be there. The beautiful worship surprised me. We sang "Shout to the North," "O Zion Haste," and "Lift High the Cross," then heard a very good sermon by a missionary, followed by a reflective Communion service. I said to myself, *I think God may want us here.*

On Mother's Day I laughed when Paul announced "We don't do 'momilies.'" I've heard enough sermons extolling motherhood. It pleased me that they stick with the most important message. And Paul gave an incredible message from Isaiah 53. "He was pierced for our transgressions, he was crushed for our iniquities, the punishment that brought us peace was upon him, and by his wounds we are healed" (Isa. 53:5). We tend to keep our faith on the surface, dwelling on love and goodness and never comprehending the depth and complexity of God's love; never seeing Jesus as despised and rejected, like a rose crushed to give us his fragrance and cover our sin.

The friendliness of Grace Church continued to surprise us. After church one Sunday we met Louise and her family. They had come from Hillcrest Church, and her children took piano from Madison. They left Hillcrest because of many changes and a lack of connection. We also talked with Paul. On the way home Mike commented on Paul's warmth. At bedtime Mike told me, "I'm coming around about Grace Church being a fit for us!"

**Introduction to Grace Church**

Mike and I attended the Grace Church introduction class. Though uncertain about joining Grace Church, we wanted to learn all we could about it. Also, the class came at a convenient time—one evening in June as opposed to four classes on Sunday mornings in the fall. The class included a light supper sitting around a table together with eight class members and the five laypeople leading it.

John and Judy chaired the class with a welcome and introductions around the table. Three elders presented information about every aspect of Grace Church, and we were given a binder with data. They described the history, constitution, and finances of the church followed by a detailed presentation on their doctrinal statement and what the gospel includes. The leaders were each knowledgeable, well prepared, and open to questions. And they connected well with us. We learned the three requirements for joining Grace Church "family"— take the introductory class, share our testimony with a designated Grace Church leader, and sign the Covenant of Fellowship.

## Doubt

After the Grace Church introductory class, Mike was still doubtful and wanted to return to Hillcrest Church. I prayed for patience and understanding and realized I also felt ambivalent. I listed in my journal the ways Grace Church was different from Hillcrest:

1. Music—All songs are praises to God, easy to sing, peaceful and inspiring. Little raising of hands, no applause (except for the children).
2. Message—verse-by-verse Bible teaching. No application, no entertaining us, no catchy series. Very deep theological ideas, beliefs, and deeply devout.
3. Prayer of confession and prayer of intercession and benediction every week with times of silence. I don't think I'll miss Hillcrest Church's scant praying.
4. Communion—Scripture read or recited with time to take Communion prayerfully and thoughtfully. Love this.
5. Observe Holy Week and Christmas in traditional ways.
6. Mission Moment describes a mission of the church each week. They know their missionaries and pray for them. No pressure to go and do.
7. Theology is affirmed by all—unity and understanding of it, strong faith.
8. Men in leadership—many!

## DISCOVERY AND LEARNING

We joined the fourteen-week summer Bible class, "Who's Who in the New," a study of New Testament characters, one each Sunday, each taught by a different teacher. The male leadership in this church is strong and plentiful.

During the summer, Pastor Paul presented a series of messages called "Understanding the Times." On June 15 he talked about pre-modernism (early twentieth century), modernism, (science will give you answers) and postmodernism. According to postmodernism, truth is not discovered, it is created; they claim there is no basis for truth! Mike was pleased with this message and very interested.

In June, I ventured to a women's Bible class on a weekday morning and to the prayer meeting in the evening and connected with many new people at Grace Church. Good participation and the presence of God's Spirit characterized both meetings. Paul led the prayer meeting, and when he prayed his bass voice reminded me of Pastor Jim. Paul is built like a bear, yet he is soft-spoken, humble, and gentle. The group prayed for missionaries they know, and prayers were specific. The women's class debated theological issues about our righteousness in Christ. Both groups amazed me!

In July, Mike told me he believes along the lines of Grace Church. We had recently read about the divisive issues in the Methodist Church. That same day, John invited Mike to play golf. He couldn't, due to a doctor appointment, but later joined the Grace Church golf group.

One Sunday in July, Paul described their church plant in Bulgaria and named the people from Grace Church visiting there. They also have a church plant locally and one in India. Paul choked up telling of the recent death of his interpreter in India. He gave an outstanding message on, "Who Am I?" It doesn't matter what we wear or what group we're in. We don't create our own truths or reality, though some think they do. We are made in the image of God. No two people are identical. God is personally acquainted with each of us. I wrote in my journal "Thank you, Lord, for this message and for Paul, our new pastor! Thank you for this church—I know we will grow here—a scary thought!"

**Hillcrest and Grace Church in One Day**

In late August, Mike and I had a heart-to-heart talk about Grace Church. Mike liked the Bible class, describing it as better than anything at Hillcrest. But he felt more comfortable with Hillcrest worship. We made plans to go to Hillcrest early service and to Grace Church second service the following Sunday.

The Hillcrest traditional service evoked a mixture of emotions and reactions. The organ music brought tears, as a new organist played with intensity and passion. Mike connected with his golf friends, and I connected with Madison and Lynn plus several other good friends, but a number of people said a casual hello without warmth or even recognition that we'd left!

Dennis (Teaching Pastor) gave a message about Jesus in the Garden of Gethsemane, using it to teach what we're to do. He listed seven things, including being in community (small group), forgiving others, and obeying God. How he got this from Luke 22:39–46 is beyond me—plus it's all things we know. I kept looking at my watch during his message.

Madison's eyes lit up with surprise when she saw us. She is a delight. Lynn said a restrained hello, but was preoccupied with registering people for ladies' Bible study. Suzy asked, "Are you coming back?" Charles and Joanne seemed very pleased to see us. Mike enjoyed Dennis and seeing his friends and felt he fit in there.

At Grace Church someone we didn't know invited us to a senior lunch after church. Another man we'd met before shook our hands. We saw Johnny from class and prayer meeting with his nose bandaged and talked with him. In the sanctuary, Louise and her family sat in front of us, and we had a good and rather long conversation. She homeschools four children ages thirteen, eleven, eight, and five. None of the Grace Church songs were familiar, but the words inspired me. They fit with Paul's message on Isaiah 55:6–13, about God's amazing forgiveness. Mike seemed bored during Paul's message about God giving his Son and his inability to be in the presence of sin—he's so holy. Some of this I didn't want to hear!

**Assimilation Dinner**

We received an invitation to the Assimilation Dinner in early September, though we had not made a decision about joining Grace Church. The comfortableness of the evening surprised us. A group of about two-dozen people came, half of them church staff or assimilation team members. We enjoyed a delicious dinner and the gathering afterward, with introductions all around the group.

The following day touched and amazed us both. Mike remarked afterward on the significance of the Communion service. I wrote in my journal, "Grace Church takes my breath away—or maybe it's giving me more breath than I'm ready for!"

## More Doubt

Our doubt and ambivalence continued as noted in my journal:

**October 2008**

> Mike and I continue to waver about Grace Church and God's will for us. I want more personal connection and more joy.

> Also the teaching is difficult. Am I struggling to surrender on another level? It seems beyond me, and I know it will change both of us. Yet all churches should (will?) do this. Mike wants more application, yet admits he didn't apply much when given it by Ted. Help us and guide us, Lord. As usual, I want this decided—so I can plan (control) my life ahead.

**Meeting with Paul**

We decided to meet with Paul to help us understand Grace Church more fully and to resolve our ambivalence. Our meeting lasted two solid hours! Paul listened patiently to us and displayed a humble spirit. Mike asked how an elder-led church operates. Paul described the elders as a very devout group of men and said they solve issues by coming to consensus, by discerning the will of God.

I told Paul how painful changing churches had been even with God leading us to do so. He said his wife's mother became very upset about issues in her church of thirty years and said, "I'm dying here." They suggested another church, and she made a change at age eighty-six. In Paul's prayer at the end, he thanked God for the encouragement that meeting with us had given him! Mike seemed pleased about this meeting, so we're moving closer to joining Grace Church.

## No Longer a Church Orphan

Two weeks after our talk with Paul, we decided to join Grace Church. Paul said we didn't need to give our witness to anyone else. I experienced an immediate lightness, like a weight lifted. This continued through the afternoon and all night. I wrote in my journal:

I'm no longer a church orphan! My security is in you, Lord, I know, but it helps to have strong, loving Christian support here on earth also. The church keeps me growing in knowing you, keeps me in a loving community, reminding me and teaching me to love and to give. I *have* to be part of the body of Christ. My heart feels warm just writing about it.

Our ambivalence about joining Grace Church sprang from the messages—true to God's Word in its entirely. Sad to say, but we heard only part of the Word at our first two churches. God's design moved us along to deeper and more complete teaching of his Word as we grew.

Each time we changed churches, the new church stretched us spiritually. We were forced to grow. We plan to stay at Grace Church and continue growing—unless God moves us again!

## Interlude

# Guide for Leavers and Leaders

## Tears and Reason

GOD CREATED WOMAN on the sixth day. A watching angel moved close and touched her.

"You made her so soft, God."

"She is soft," God agreed, "but she is also tough."

"Will she be able to think?" asked the angel.

"Oh yes, she'll be able to think and reason very well."

The angel touched the woman's cheek and said, "Oops, it looks like you have a leak in this model."

"That's not a leak; those are tears."

"What are tears for?" the angel asked.

The Lord said, "Tears are her way of expressing joy, sorrow, pain, disappointment, love, loneliness, and grief. She's full of emotions she needs to share, but she can also think."

### Understanding Grief, Loss, and Leaving a Church

You have read our story, including the raw details of my tears and emotions through our church trials, doubts, and changes. I hope readers facing painful church issues will realize they are not alone or crazy or wrong in their own tears, frustration, ambivalence, depression, and anger. Our feelings enliven our humanness. They come and go and can't be relied on alone. But they play a valuable role, and we need to pay attention to them. Men have tears also. "Jesus wept"(John 11:35). Tears are an important part of every human being's nature, not just a female trait.

We need to pay attention to reason and facts also. But reason and facts alone can be cold and barren. Our feelings inform our reason and vice versa. When we deny or suppress our feelings, they creep out in covert ways. Awareness of our feelings enables us to grieve losses and be authentic. We aren't as rational as we think! To heal and grow, we need to express our feelings, learn from them, and then let go of them.

This Interlude between Part 1 and Part 2 gives an overview of the struggling, grieving, searching, leaving, joining, and assimilating process—the road traveled when a Christian switches churches. I hope this brief explanatory section will be helpful to leavers and leaders.

## Understanding Church Hoppers

All of us, pastors, elders, and church members, need to understand church hoppers. Based on Lifeway research, 76 percent of church hoppers are mature Christians who leave for valid reasons, who do so prayerfully. What about the other 24 percent? We must not judge them. We are all works in progress.

By hindsight, I see that our status as "church hoppers" contributed to the detachment or disconnect between us and Pastor Ted. In researching this book, I learned many pastors and church leaders look down on people who switch churches.

"I always approached these people with some skepticism and caution," said Brad Waggoner, a pastor and the author of the Lifeway study. "I would wonder why they were leaving and what they were looking for. Would they stick any better at our church? Were they bringing any toxic attitudes with them?" Waggoner now realizes most of these switchers "became very solid, healthy, and active members." Waggoner's study on church switchers showed the majority of the people who switch churches are mature believers and an asset to the church.[1]

Waggoner's skepticism astonished me. I thought pastors would understand this phenomenon. I thought they would give more grace than I tended to give. I had judged people who switched from one church to another until I became one. Hopefully the Lifeway study has slowed down the swift judgment of church switchers. Most leavers are hurt, angry, or disappointed by a church they loved and supported for years. The majority of church switchers change churches for valid biblical reasons.

## GRIEVING

The pain of leaving a church is excruciating. Church ties are not easily severed. Leaving a church cuts leavers off—separates them from the local body of believers. I'm defining "leavers" as those in the process of leaving—first thinking about it, then praying about it, finally deciding—over a period of time.

The process of leaving follows the five stages of grief, though not necessarily in the same order, and each stage may be revisited again. The process takes time and varies with each leaver. These are the stages:

1. Denial—"This can't be happening." Leavers feel numb; they deny the issues and avoid talking about them. They put on a fake smile and pretend all is okay. Leavers may even convince themselves nothing is bothering them.

2. Anger—"I'm angry about what's happened to cause this." Leavers feel angry about hurtful or abusive experiences, disruptive changes, and disagreements or disappointment with members or leaders. Anger may be easier for some to express than the hurt hidden behind it. The anger may or may not be for valid reasons. Emotions are, by definition, not rational. When church leaders fail to teach the truth, or when they instigate changes without attempting to maintain unity, anger is valid. Changes that veer the church off course (pragmatic changes rather than prayerful ones) give reason for anger.
3. Bargaining—"I won't have to leave if ... ?" The leaving member dreams of scenarios to delay or prevent the inevitable loss. The pain of losing their entire church family hurts terribly. Many wait out a pastor or bargain with God—praying for the pastor to leave or for the problem to go away.
4. Depression—Leaving members feel extremely sad about their loss. Tearful laments define this stage. Leaving, though scary, may be a relief at this point. Depression can continue beyond leaving.
5. Acceptance—Leavers who find another church eventually accept their loss. They move on to a new church family. Later they realize their painful loss led to personal growth. We grow from our struggles.

## Navigating the Grieving Process

Here are four steps to help leavers navigate the grieving process.

**Hang on to your faith.**

Spend more time than ever in prayer and Bible study while grieving. Pain and struggle usually bring us to our knees—for good reason. God is our hope in time of trouble (Psalm 46:1). Don't let bitterness, anger, or fear of your emotions overflowing keep you from leaning on God and his Word.

**Journal about your loss.**

Writing enables leavers to process experiences, thoughts, and feelings, and let go. Leavers, I challenge you to write for twenty to thirty minutes about troubling church experiences. Do this without censoring your writing. Repeat three to five days in a row. Describe in detail your concerns and painful emotions. You can write letters or make lists of grievances. Save your writing and reread it later to gain perspective. *Do not send* an emotion-packed letter. It will make things worse. Writing about painful issues takes courage. Grab yourself by the scruff of the neck and make yourself do it. Continue to write and pray throughout your struggle, tears, questions, and doubts. I guarantee it will help.

**Look outside for support.**

While still involved in the church you're leaving—unable to be open, unable to worship, gripped with grief—look for outside help. Parachurch groups outside your church can be a life raft in the storm. Look for prayer groups, Bible studies, and worship services. Our contacts with Emmaus, the prayer group, and a Bible study elsewhere anchored us through the grieving and struggling at Main Street Church.

**Seek professional help.**

If pain persists, counseling can help. One session of counseling from a pastor in a nearby city was invaluable to me during my struggles about Edna. Choose a Christian counselor, knowledgeable about church and the Christian worldview.

## VALID REASON FOR LEAVING

Valid reasons for leaving are listed below and need to be considered prayerfully.

**Your church is led by a false teacher.**

False teachers are not easy to spot. Biblical words camouflage their counterfeit beliefs. Is the name of Jesus exalted? Is Scripture taught in context and believed? Are New Age beliefs mingled with Christian teaching? False teachers say biblical words, but modify the context or meaning. Casual Christians, seekers, and those new to belief may not know the essentials of the faith.

I hope readers will study the Word and learn to spot false teachers. Read Scripture on false teaching to discern truth and remember, "Satan himself masquerades as an angel of light" (2 Cor. 11:14). Strong lay leadership in a church can hold both clergy and laity accountable to God and his Word. Main Street Church lacked this.

**Your church neglects important doctrinal issues.**

The Apostles' Creed and the Nicene Creed summarize the basic Christian doctrines. God, the Father Almighty, is the Creator of heaven and earth. Jesus is the Son of God. He lived a sinless life, died for our sins, and arose from the dead. Belief in the trinity—Father, Son, and Holy Spirit—and Scripture as the Word of God are primary doctrines. We are sinners saved by faith in Christ Jesus—redeemed by his blood. The neglect of essential doctrines, or a bending or blending of them, gives valid reason to leave a church.

**Your church overlooks flagrant sins by leaders.**

Sexual sins inflict great damage to congregations. Sadly, some pastors and leaders have carried on affairs or abused children. Some have been addicted to drugs or alcohol, stolen church money, been deceivers, liars, manipulators. Many pastors today do not support traditional marriage. Each local church needs a process for holding leaders and members accountable to the church and to God. Unfortunately, many churches lack accountability; are led and controlled by one pastor. Also many churches are dominated by the requirements and biases of the hierarchy with beliefs and values contrary to that of the congregation and, more importantly, contrary to the Word of God.

**God calls you to a ministry at another church.**

Leavers who sense God's call to a ministry at another church have a valid reason for leaving. Jane and Douglas, friends at Hillcrest, left when they sensed God's call to help plant a Nazarene church nearby. They arrived at this idea independent of each other—a verification of God's call.

**A lengthy conflict in your church remains unresolved.**

A church division hurts the entire church. A prolonged conflict stalls spiritual growth and saps the vitality of members. Strong, mature Christians may be able to stay the course. New Christians better not risk it. The Methodist Church continues in a decades-long struggle between the liberal hierarchy and the conservative members. The Confessing Movement lovingly holds the church accountable to its professed doctrines and policies. I admire the tenacity of this group. Mike and I, regretfully, could not stay the course. Our faith was too new and fragile to risk it. God calls some to stay and some to leave.

**Changes accommodating the culture are adopted.**

The most blatant accommodation to the culture is the acceptance of same sex "marriage." Less obvious is the use of secular marketing methods to build the size of the church. This is often driven by human measures of success rather than by prayer and concern for unity.

**You believe you won't grow spiritually at your present church.**

The above issues may stunt your spiritual growth if you stay. No matter the reasons, the decision must be covered in prayer and not made lightly.

## Steps toward Leaving

The leaving process requires time, thought, and prayer. Leaving is gradual, like stepping-stones to a destination. Here are steps to guide your leave-taking.

**Pray about God's will for you.**

Seek God's will with all your heart. Valid reasons for leaving may apply to your church, but God may call some away and call others to stay. Even when you are certain about leaving, pray about his timing. At both Main Street Church and Hillcrest Church, we waited more than a year after the difficulties began. I believed staying would stunt our spiritual growth or worse. I drifted away from God once and couldn't risk that again. Others stayed as led by God. Take your time. Ask God to help you discern his will. Read Scripture for guidance.

**Write your thoughts and prayers.**

Writing about a confusing or painful issue will help you process your thoughts and feelings and let go of hurt and anger. It will also help you understand the issues, give you insight, and help you discern God's will.

**Keep a balanced view of the church you're leaving.**

No church is perfect. Your belief that you can't grow in your present church doesn't mean others who remain will be unable to grow. Also, those who stay are still your brothers and sisters in Christ. God leads each person in a unique way for a variety of reasons.

**Keep a balanced view of the pastor you're leaving.**

No pastor is perfect. Pastors follow God's call and follow the truth as they know it. Some lack education, some hold misguided beliefs, some compromise the message to win postmoderns, and some carry baggage from the past. They are human (sinners) and need to be given grace. They have a difficult job. Pray for them.

**Talk about the decision with your spouse.**

Couples need to dialogue with each other about the reasons for leaving. Share your dissatisfactions and your perceptions of God's will. One may believe God wants you to stay, and the other may sense God leading you elsewhere. Pray for unity between you. Couples also need to discuss what leaving will mean in terms of friendships and connections.

**Be patient with each other and be good listeners.**

If you can't talk to each other with acceptance and love, write out your views and share what you've written. Then see if you can talk. If this doesn't help, meet together with a trusted friend or pastor outside the church.

**Tell church leaders about your discontent.**

Speak lovingly, respectfully, and honestly with your leaders about the details of your dissatisfaction. Tell it in person and in writing, and send your letter or e-mail to more than one person. They need to know.

**Find someone you can talk with about the problems.**

See a pastor, Stephen Minister, or counselor outside the church if you are deeply troubled.

**Forgive those who have let you down or hurt you.**

Let go of grudges and bitterness—forgive! Keeping a prayer journal will help. Talk to God honestly about your thoughts, needs, and feelings, and don't blame him.

**Tell friends and classes or groups.**

If you decide to leave, let friends and acquaintances know about it. Closure helps everyone. People will miss you and vice versa, and you may find ways to continue some of these friendships. Be cautious in explaining your *reasons* for leaving to avoid sowing discontent.

**Allow yourself to grieve the loss.**

Face your feelings—especially anger and hurt. Change is difficult, and our emotions by definition are not rational. Accept your feelings, express them safely, and give them to God.

## Searching

Searching for another church is an education and an adventure. Here are the steps we took and an elaboration of our experiences while searching.

**Plan your search.**

When we left Main Street Church, we visited two American Baptist churches, three Methodist churches and the Vineyard, all located in our small town, before finding Hillcrest Church in the city. In prior years we had visited two local Presbyterian churches and one local Episcopal church with visiting family members. We knew many of the members of these churches and some of the pastors, so we knew the options well.

When we left Hillcrest, Mike and I pondered at length what kind of church we hoped to find. We agreed we wanted a biblical church that exalted Christ. We hoped for a friendly church with reverent worship, good music, and a deliberate Communion service. Any church with these qualities we assumed would also be mission- and outreach-minded. We narrowed our search to churches nearby (a ten- or fifteen-minute drive), so we could be active at any age. We hoped to find a smaller church, making it easier to meet and know others.

**Gather information.**

Websites and recommendations from friends you trust can help steer your search. We studied the websites of a variety of churches before making a list of churches to visit. We ruled out three nearby churches—Presbyterian, Episcopal, and Assembly of God—due to prior experiences or information from others. A former youth leader at Main Street, now a pastor, told us about the two most biblical Methodist churches. (At that point we were looking for a supplemental church and we had fond memories of Methodist worship. We didn't expect to join another Methodist church because of the apostasy in the hierarchy.)

**Take notes.**

Each time we visited a new church, we rated it as to location, facility, friendliness, worship service, prayers, music, and message. It helps to write down comments for future reference, especially if you visit several churches. It's important to note your objective and subjective reactions to the church. Were you inspired or touched? Did you learn something from the message? Were you able to truly worship? Did you connect with anyone?

**Pray—and notice the Spirit's leading.**

Another factor we noticed was the presence of God in the worship. This is vitally important. Sensing the presence of God is spiritually discerned. If you prayerfully approach each church you visit, I believe the Holy Spirit will touch you, showing you this is your new church. And this will happen repeatedly as you visit again and again.

**Friendliness is worth noting.**

The friendliness of church members gave clues to their acceptance of strangers. Greeters at the doors and in the welcome centers helped us open up. The arrangement of the space made a difference; some entrances were very crowded with little room to mingle. A greeting time during the service helped visitors and members connect and enabled church members to note newcomers near them. Grace Church regularly asks people to pass the attendance pad down the pew, and as it comes back, to note the names of newcomers. The church we visited with unused name tags on their bulletins failed in their attempt at being friendly. Openness can't be faked or pressured by the leadership. It must be real.

Each person we met expanded our view of the church. Each contact added to our comfort, eased our stranger anxiety, and educated us about the church. Our first Sunday at Grace Church, we met a school counselor from our granddaughter's school. She introduced herself, recognized our last name, and asked questions. I clammed up at first, but Mike responded, and we then connected comfortably. A friend from Bible Study Fellowship greeted Mike the second time we went to Grace Church. Weeks later, we asked for information at the welcome center and met a bubbly, outgoing woman who volunteered helpful information about the church and personal information about herself and the pastor. As seekers, we were hungry for information.

## JOINING

The Holy Spirit touched us so profoundly on our first visit to Main Street Church we had no doubt about joining. Coming from secular beliefs (unbelief, really), we might have delayed joining if they had required us to profess belief in Jesus as our Lord and Savior.

The long commute to Hillcrest Church made us uncertain about joining. The first summer, as we commuted back and forth, I prayed repeatedly, *Lord, do you really want us to drive this far to church?* By the end of the summer we were hooked on the church, pleased it was my Dad's denomination, and located close to our children. God gave us astounding additional verification— the discovery that our wedding occurred in this church in a prior location.

Our ambivalence and uncertainty about Grace Church made the decision to join slow and difficult. The reason: God led us in a totally unexpected direction—not geographically, but quite a leap in worship style, church organization, and doctrine.

Just as grieving and leaving is a process, so is joining. Go through it prayerfully. Here are the steps:

**Expect ambivalence.**

Changing churches is similar to moving to a foreign country. You will experience culture shock, and will need to adjust to the differences. In each move, we experienced periods of ambivalence—strong attraction to the church mixed with great uncertainty and doubt. Ambivalence has two sides. Each change challenged our comfort zone, stretching us. And each church thrilled us with reminders of previous worship experiences.

**Be patient.**

Husbands and wives must practice patience with each other. Praying about your decision individually and together will keep you listening for God's will. Talking about each Sunday's experience, keeping records, and journaling helped us clarify our thoughts and understand each other's views. If you have questions about the church, make an appointment to talk with the pastor. This helped us make the decision to join.

**Be open and be active.**

All three of the churches "adopted" us into the family, each in a unique way. As visitors at Main Street Church, we connected over dinner with Pastor Wesley and his wife, Nan. The new members' class and adult Bible class welcomed us eagerly. Potluck dinners with inspirational and fun activities also bonded us with the church family.

Assimilation into a large church takes time, effort, and an atmosphere of friendliness. On one of our first Sundays at Hillcrest Church, Will approached us, introduced himself, and invited us to his Sunday-school class. We remained active in this class for six of our seven years at Hillcrest Church. We knew these friends well. The couples in the weekly marriage group also became close friends. Our deepest connections at Hillcrest were in our weekly small group with people who lived nearby.

At Grace Church, many people linger and chat before and after every service and reach out to newcomers. The introductory class and the assimilation dinner were informative, comfortable, and introduced us to others. The Sunday Bible classes helped us understand the church culture and connected us weekly. We are now in a small group at Grace Church, we attend prayer meetings, and Mike is in the golf group.

Join a class or interest group, and attend extra church functions. Don't depend on the church to make all the effort to integrate you. Newcomers must do some reaching out. Joining a class or interest group connects you with members of the church and gives you more information about how the church operates and what they believe. It takes time to know a new church. It also takes time to trust new "friends." We all have unconscious, protective walls up with strangers until we find out whether they accept us and like us and whether we "fit in" with them and with the new church. Give yourself time.

### CONNECTIONS AFTER LEAVING

After leaving Hillcrest, we stayed in our small group with a mix of members from other churches. We didn't tell group members about leaving Hillcrest, confiding only in the hosts, Madison and Buzz. Some members were young Christians, and we didn't want to influence them against Hillcrest. This weekly contact, with Christians we knew well, anchored us while we struggled through finding another church. Mike also continued in the Hillcrest golf group.

Our friends at Hillcrest and at Main Street Church expressed sadness at our leaving. Some in the Bible class at Main Street Church must have felt abandoned. We have kept in touch with Dick and Jan who led the class and with Bill and June and several others. And we have seen friends from Main Street Church at funerals and social gatherings since then. The same has been true at Hillcrest Church. I continued in Bible study through the spring of 2009. Returning to a church after you have left is disconcerting. You're a visitor in a place where you once belonged. Leaving a church tears apart church families in the same way that divorce tears apart families. It can't be done lightly, only as a last resort and with God's leading.

We have also stayed in touch with Wesley and Nan, meeting for lunch once a year or so, and we've stayed in touch with Jim and Shirley via email to Arizona. These pastors have a special place in our hearts.

## Hope for the Mainline Churches

Though we didn't return to a mainline church, we are hopeful those churches will heal their doctrinal divisions and see revival. This may be happening already. Those currently thinking of leaving may want to rethink this in light of a well-documented study of renewal movements in the Methodist, Presbyterian, Episcopal, American Baptist, Lutheran, and United Church of Christ churches. These churches, after struggling for decades to change their own denominations, are now working together and growing in numbers. The liberal hierarchies, in control for decades, are crumbling financially and otherwise. Thomas Oden, the author of the study, says, "It has taken over a quarter-century for these evangelical movements to emerge with one voice. They have all faced dismissive resistance within their own mainline denominations. They are now flourishing with growing vitality in the length and breadth of the mainline denominations."[2]

Renewal groups, previously underreported by denominational and secular media, were featured in a *Christianity Today* article called "Turning the Mainline Around." The article reports that thirty renewal groups "are revitalizing worship, reviving evangelism, and reforming the theology of mainline churches." In addition, "the strongest support for the renewal movements is among clergy under age forty-nine, while clergy nearing retirement are least supportive." And, "contrary to folk wisdom and traditional sociological theory, the mainline Protestant denominations may be poised for a historic change—a return to orthodox Christianity."[3] This is certainly encouraging news.

## Stay or Go—But Do Grow

Leaving a church is scary. It upsets our usual routines. We may decide it's easier to stay where we are. At Main Street Church, some members of the adult Bible Class recommended waiting out a pastor who was inadequate, ineffective, or not to our liking (or a false teacher?). Pastors were appointed and often didn't stay more than a few years. Mark Dever, in his book *Nine Marks of a Healthy Church*, describes a church member named Rob who disliked his pastor. He decided he would wait him out, knowing many pastors don't last long. Dever says, "Would it surprise you if I told you that Rob wasn't really growing as a Christian? And, more than that, it didn't really bother him that he wasn't growing as a Christian?"[4]

It should bother us if we're not growing. We shouldn't settle for apathy, whether we stay where we are or find another church. Beth Moore, in her *Patriarchs* study, says Abraham had to leave Ur before God would show him where he wanted him to go. Moore suggests God calls us to leave UR—an acronym for our Usual Routine. She says, "God calls us to leave our familiar spiritual countryside—our ruts, our comfort zones, and every hint of mediocrity—and 'go' to a place He will show us. Let's not settle for Haran [part way]. Let's go the distance."[5]

When God is leading you, go the distance. It will be worth it.

# Part 2

# Lessons For Changing Churches

## Get Ready

ABE LINCOLN AND a man named Berry owned a store about to go bankrupt. Discouragement ate at them. Lincoln stroked a fifty-cent piece in his pocket, his only cash. He said to Berry: "I want to study law. If I could sell everything and have enough left to buy Blackstone's *Common English Law*, I would be satisfied."

Later that day a wagon came into town and stopped there. A man hopped down and entered the store. He greeted Lincoln and said, "I'm moving my family west and running out of money. I have an empty barrel I'll sell for fifty cents." Lincoln didn't want the barrel, but feeling sorry him, gave him his last fifty cents.

The rest of the day Berry kidded Lincoln about his foolishness in buying an empty barrel. Late in the afternoon Lincoln walked to the porch, saw some papers in the barrel, and reached a long arm to the bottom. He came up with a book, Blackstone's *Common English Law*. Lincoln stood holding the book, looking toward heaven and thought, *God is showing me he has something for me to do, and I'd better get ready for it.*

God has given the church a Book and has something for the church to do, and we'd better get ready for it. He provides the way, just as he did with Lincoln.

Part 2 is a primer on church life, stressing the need for church unity, correct teaching, accountability, and commitment. Our story and the wisdom of experts weaves throughout, educating readers about the ways churches have changed and are changing. Information about the seeker church and the emerging church, about pragmatism, narcissism, and relativism in our culture and in the church, are included. There is much we need to understand.

Part 2 also offers proven biblical solutions for building up the church. We must confess our sin, repent, and change directions. We must be transformed. We must be witnesses and servants, living the "love one another" Scriptures.

My hope is that readers will prayerfully use what is helpful, prayerfully question what doesn't fit your situation, and prayerfully read from my endnotes to learn more. Let God always be your guide in this.

We must stop eminent-domain changes with prayer-filled commitment to unity in Christ. The church at its best is God's instrument to transform us. With transformational churches, the term "casual Christian" will be an oxymoron. Pansy churches will become Lily of the Valley churches.

Chapter 8

# Ideas for the Sheep

## "Bind Us Together, Lord"

To dwell in love with saints above, why that will be glory. To dwell below with saints I know, why, that's a different story.

—Anonymous

In Christ we who are many form one body, and each member belongs to all the others.

—Romans 12:5

### A Loving Connection

SHE THOUGHT HER independence and common sense protected her from falling in love too quickly. Yet after just eight weeks, she made a commitment to the Methodist. She'd spent time with a Baptist in her younger days, but they'd drifted apart. After that she avoided all relationships. They weren't for her; she didn't need them.

Oh, there were opportunities. She'd met another Baptist, two Presbyterians, and two Episcopalians over the years. They were all in her town. However, after one lackluster date with each, she had no inclination to continue any of these relationships.

When she met the Methodist, it was love at first sight. Her reaction shocked her. Usually she was cautious and methodical, but many things about the Methodist hooked her. He obviously took good care of himself; he was well-dressed and handsomely built. He planned their meetings carefully, with much attention to details. Their weekly meetings were mystical, full of joy and reverence.

She enjoyed his musical talent. He played a variety of instruments to perfection and sang beautifully. He even encouraged her to sing along. She realized music had been missing from her life for a long time. She liked the Methodist's conversation and his genuine faith in a loving God. He lived his strong beliefs. He expressed warmth and friendliness without being pushy. He paid attention to her without crowding her, and without pressuring her for a commitment.

She compared him to the others she'd met. Some were bland, lifeless, or boring; others were stifling or judgmental. She compared him to the Baptist she'd loved so much in her younger years and realized how much she'd missed that joyous, loving connection.

So, here she was in eight short weeks, already committing herself to the Methodist. Was this true love? Would this infatuation last? She knew the honeymoon stage wouldn't last. She would learn about the Methodist's flaws, and he would learn about hers. But she was sure their love would grow and deepen.

God's love drew us. That's why we joined Main Street United Methodist Church on May 6, 1990. God draws, pulls, hauls, or drags Christians to himself, to his church, and to the love of brothers and sisters in Christ. When we fall in love with Jesus, we also fall in love with his church. Our loving connection with a church expands, enriches, and cements our loving connection with God.

This chapter focuses on the role members share in building up the local church—the church where God has placed us. We'll briefly consider how to create a loving church connection, one that keeps us growing in Christ.

### BUILDING UP THE CHURCH WHERE YOU ARE

The church is the body of Christ. It's the place where his Spirit dwells on earth. Some churches are bland, lifeless, judgmental, or stifling. Some are boring. Some are beautiful, well cared for, accepting, and welcoming. Some transform us. Some are true to Christ and his presence is obviously there. His presence is what draws us and changes us.

What makes the difference? The church is made up of all kinds of people. Some of us are bland, lifeless, judgmental, stifling, or boring. All of us are sinners. Scripture compares us to sheep, with Christ as the Good Shepherd. Sheep—the members of the church—are dumb and dirty. Scripture says we are also part of a royal priesthood. How can dirty, dumb sheep be priests? Christ loves us, cleanses us, grows us, and uses us. We are transformed by Jesus' amazing grace—from caterpillars to butterflies, from sheep to royal priests.

The priesthood of all believers is a biblical concept describing the role of the laity in the church. Each of us is a minister or a priest to the world in Christ's name. All believers are called and given authority to be instruments of God's grace in people's lives. We share in this priesthood, in partnership with Christ. The idea that only clergy do ministry and the laity are consumers of it is unbiblical. This is how it is expressed in Scripture:

> As you come to him, the living Stone—rejected by men but chosen by God and precious to him—you also, like living stones, are being built into a spiritual house to be a holy

> priesthood, offering spiritual sacrifices acceptable to God through Jesus Christ. . . . You are a chosen people, a royal priesthood, a holy nation, a people belonging to God, that you may declare the praises of him who called you out of darkness into his wonderful light. Once you were not a people, but now you are the people of God; once you had not received mercy, but now you have received mercy.
>
> —1 Peter 2:4–5, 9–10

We have a serious and a sacred obligation to build up our local church. We must give up our sheepish ways and act as priests to one another. How do we do this? Let's look at some specific suggestions.

**Be Committed**

Ask yourself, *What kind of church would my church be if every member were just like me?* The church needs dedicated, committed, caring members who have given their lives to Christ. Do you know Jesus as your Lord and Savior? Has your life been transformed? Are you "a new creation" in Christ (2 Cor. 5:17)? Jesus said, "No one can see the kingdom of God unless he is born again" (John 3:3). He also said, "Whoever believes in the Son has eternal life, but whoever rejects the Son will not see life, for God's wrath remains on him" (John 3:36), and "I am the way and the truth and the life. No one comes to the Father except through me" (John 14:6).

The teaching is very clear. He is the only way. We need a heart change, a bending of our will to his will, an inner transformation. If you haven't experienced a true change of heart, pray to receive Christ. Give your life to him. Give him permission to create in you a new heart, to change you. We need to recommit our lives to him daily.

### Study the Word of God

The Bible is the holy Word of God. Do you read and study God's Word on a daily basis? We need a clear grasp of the Bible to understand what it teaches. The Bible reveals the character of God showing us he is holy, omnipotent, trustworthy, and personal. He is working out his plan through Christ Jesus. The Bible feeds our faith, guides our walk, and gives us hope. We need to ramp up our study of God's Word.

### Forgive Others

Do you hold grudges? Is there someone you "can't" forgive? Jesus commands us to forgive not seven times, but seventy times seven (Matt. 18:22). We must forgive those who hurt us no matter how often they offend us. Holding on to unforgiveness is like drinking poison and hoping it will hurt the other person! A lack of forgiveness infects our souls and is a sin. God forgives us and gives us grace. We must forgive others.

### Pray Daily

Prayer and worship are essential in the life of a Christian. These, plus God's Word, connect us with God. When we pray, we admit our powerlessness, humbling ourselves before God. We place our faith in him. The prayer life of Jesus shows his dependence on God. Jesus *often* withdrew to lonely places and prayed (Luke 5:16). If he needed to pray, certainly we do.

Paul tells us to "pray continually" (1 Thess. 5:17). This is a challenge! If we pray when we first wake up, pray before each meal, and pray at bedtime, we can come closer to fulfilling Paul's admonition to pray continually. Prayer changes us, grows us. A daily time of prayer is essential to our Christian walk. "A prayer-less Christian is like a bus driver trying alone to push his bus out of a rut because he doesn't know Clark Kent is on board."[1] God is with us. When we ignore him, it's similar to ignoring a good friend who is right in the room with us.

### Pray for and Appreciate Pastors

Pastors perform a variety of tasks and are on call, day in and day out. My father wrote ambivalently, "I'm excited about my first church, but it's hard to imagine giving up my Sundays and my weekends for the rest of my life." Pastors follow a different schedule than most of us. They give up their weekends and their holidays—because they're working. They're in demand at odd hours—when people are sick, when tragedy strikes, and on happy occasions like weddings. Often their family life is slighted.

Pastors also suffer from the apathy of members. Parents who pour their hearts into their children know how it hurts when their children are indifferent. This is also true for pastors. John MacArthur says, "The toughest thing to deal with in the ministry is indifference."[2] Spurgeon, in the late nineteenth century, said the same thing, "Everywhere there is apathy. Nobody cares whether that which is preached is true or false. A sermon is a sermon whatever the subject; only, the shorter it is the better."[3]

Pastors and leaders are under attack from needy or disgruntled church members. They can't possibly meet the expectations of every member, and Satan also is after them! Members, respect, value, and love your pastors, and pray for them. Put them on your daily prayer list.

### Eliminate Gossip and Criticism

Negative talk about the church and its leaders needs to stop. Pastors are the target of much petty criticism. My father wrote:

> I went to visit Hanson. Long talk. Tells me much criticism of me currently. My clothes, Martha's clothes, lack of sympathy, radical sermons, music, and retreats. Almost anything and everything criticized. What to do? I know only two things.
> 1. Face it.
> 2. Pray.

At the bottom of the page he wrote and underlined: "Headache."

Criticism and gossip hurt the church. James, the brother of Jesus, writes, "The tongue is a small part of the body, but it makes great boasts. Consider what a great forest is set on fire by a small spark. The tongue also is a fire, a world of evil among the parts of the body. It corrupts the whole person, sets the whole course of his life on fire, and is itself set on fire by hell" (James 3:5–6). These are strong words. What we say to others can burn and even destroy.

We need to pray before speaking a criticism. An issue detrimental to the church should be brought to the attention of the pastors, elders, or persons involved. Don't spread gossip—go to the source, and clear it up. Most gossip is petty. Most criticisms are petty. Don't sweat the small stuff.

We need to respond to gossip and criticism by lovingly stopping it. If someone blurts out criticisms or gossip about the church or pastor, we can reply, "I'm sorry you feel this way. I urge you to share this with the pastor or an elder."

If you don't think gossip hurts the church, check out Romans 1:29–31, a passage that lumps the sin of gossip with murder, strife, deceit, malice, and arrogance. We need to realize criticism and gossip offend God, his church, and his pastors, leaving a blemish on the church. We need to ask God to change our hearts, so we will speak encouragement and affirmation often, and speak the truth in love when necessary.

### Offer Encouragement

Give seven times as much positive feedback as negative. We can regularly share the positive impact of a pastor's message or a teacher's lesson in a quick e-mail. I wish I had done this more with Pastor Ted at Hillcrest Church. Share yourself with other members of the church as well as those in leadership. Everyone has times of discouragement, stress, sickness, or tragedy. Send cards, call with support, be a friend in the good times as well as the bad times.

### Support Your Church

Give your time, your presence, your gifts, and your service to your local church. Many helpers are needed. Opportunities to contribute to the growth and health of your church abound. It's not about do, do, do. It's about giving your heart to Christ and being transformed—becoming a new creation in Christ. We are no longer bland, lifeless, judgmental, stifling, or boring. Our hearts are on fire with the love of Christ. We long to share it with others, and we long to serve him. For the church to be transformed, we need to have radical faith and never stop growing.

While praying, I had a vision of my church lit up like a Thomas Kinkade painting. It reminded me of a scene in *Piercing the Darkness*, a novel by Frank Peretti, in which angels and demons battle in the heavenlies over a small town. When the church prayed, the angels won the battles hands down. Prayer is powerful. Committed Christians worshipping, praying, studying his Word—being the church together—are powerful. We affect the outcome of heavenly and earthly battles! The building is not the church. We are the church. May Christ's light shine brightly in our lives.

CHAPTER 9

# IDEAS FOR THE SHEPHERDS
## "I LOVE TO TELL THE STORY"

> One of the most devastating causes of erosion in the church has been the drift of pastors from the bold proclamation of God's Word.
>
> —Chuck Swindoll

> Keep watch over yourselves and all the flock of which the Holy Spirit has made you overseers. Be shepherds of the church of God, which he bought with his own blood.
>
> —Acts 20:28

### I AM THE GOOD BOSS—A MODERN PARAPHRASE OF JOHN 10:11–16

I AM THE good boss, I care about my employees. They do their jobs with my support, guidance, and protection. I extend myself to meet their needs.

Dilbert and Enron bosses don't care. They're unfair, immoral, and self-centered. They care only about the bottom line. When the corporate raiders come, a Dilbert or Enron boss protects only himself. He takes his golden parachute and flies away, leaving the employees vulnerable to layoffs. He cares only about himself.

I am the good boss; I know my employees, and they know me. Because I care, we work in unity and can ward off the Dilberts, the Enrons, and the corporate raiders of the world. Yet, I care about them, too.

## Caveat to the Shepherds

I offer these ideas thoughtfully, prayerfully, and with love in my heart for pastors, elders, deacons, and leaders called by God to shepherd Christ's church. I love the church, and I love pastors. My father, grandfather, and a brother-in-law were pastors—all now with the Lord. In addition, I have been taught, counseled, and served by a number of pastors, youth leaders, and Christian college leaders prior to the five pastors in this book.

## The Good Shepherd's Job Description

Pastors are to shepherd the church (Acts 20:28). John Stott, in *The Contemporary Christian*, lists seven ways the good shepherd cares for his sheep. I have excerpted some of his ideas and added Scripture and my own comments. Some of these will be elaborated on in subsequent chapters.

**The good shepherd knows his sheep.**

"I am the good shepherd; I know my sheep and my sheep know me" (John 10:14). John Stott says church members, "are not our clients, constituents, patients, or customers. Still less are they names on a register or worse still, numbers on a computer card. Instead they are individual persons, whom we know and who know us."[1]

When we returned to church, I yearned for a close connection with the pastor. The tie to God as Father helped, but being known by a pastor "with skin on" healed deep wounds. My first two pastors, Wesley and Jim, put effort and care into knowing their sheep. They shook hands after each service, visited members, taught classes, and the personalities of both were outgoing, affirming, and upbeat.

The size of Hillcrest made it difficult for Ted to know all his sheep, though he remembered names and gave verbal greetings. Ted has a reserved personality, hindering close ties. Paul's warmth and openness became apparent as we attended prayer meetings he led and classes he taught. The strong elder leadership at Grace Church spread the task of knowing the flock, giving the sheep added assurance. In an impersonal world, being known by a pastor is deeply reassuring.

**The good shepherd serves his sheep.**

"The good shepherd lays down his life for the sheep" (John 10:11). A pastor is called to give of himself for the flock. His life is consumed with serving. Pastors must connect and work with all kinds of people. They face a variety of demands and expectations. Some Christians are not very Christ-like. Some are self-centered, pushy, angry, blaming, and controlling. Some have problems—marital issues, depression, mental illness, and unemployment. They come from all walks of life and in all ages and conditions. Pastors are human and can't be all things to all people.

Even so, pastors should guard against favoring the young and the healthy middle class, and ignoring the singles, elderly, poor, and infirm. We have much to learn from each person and each generation. We need to know each other. The beauty of the church lies in the fact that it spans the generations like a family.

**The good shepherd leads his sheep.**

"He calls his own sheep by name and leads them out. When he has brought out all his own, he goes on ahead of them, and his sheep follow him because they know his voice" (John 10:3–4). Pastors must have a clear biblical vision for their church, and they must possess the tenacity to lead the sheep, keeping them unified. The focus of the church must be first and foremost on God in Christ Jesus, seeking his will and glorifying him. The pastor must aim to please God, not the sheep.

The good shepherd leads with openness and transparency; with no secrets plans. Picture an elephant in the living room. Family members walk around it, ignoring it. Dysfunctional families keep secrets this way. Healthy families are open with each other and have no secrets. The same is true for healthy churches.

Calvin Miller, author and pastor, describes the best advice he ever received. A church member told him:

> Never have any special group in your church who knows the critical ins and outs of your dreams, while the bulk of the people are in the dark.... Keep every plan out in the open, and you'll never get in trouble. Keep the church finances that way too. Let everybody know freely everything you know, and don't have any special people you try to placate by giving them information first. When everybody owns the church and its dreams, the church is healthy. When there are little secret pockets of informants, decay is in the wind.[2]

We need healthy, open churches.

**The good shepherd feeds his sheep.**

Stott says, "Too many congregations are sick and even starving for lack of the 'solid food' of the Word of God."[3] In other words, pastors must teach the Word of God. Scripture supports this, "Man does not live on bread alone, but on every word that comes from the mouth of God" (Matt. 4:4). "Sanctify them by the truth; your word is truth" (John 17:17). "Your word is a lamp to my feet and a light for my path" (Ps. 119:105).

We were blessed. All three churches and four of our five pastors did preach, teach, and uphold the basic doctrines of the faith, including the virgin birth, the incarnation of Jesus Christ, his miracles of healing, his magnificent teaching, his sacrificial death on the cross, and his resurrection from the dead. Each church met us where we were in our faith and knowledge and stretched us with new learning and insight. The only exception was Edna, a false teacher. She pulled the wool over the eyes of the biblically illiterate sheep.

Some pastors compromise the gospel by omitting some of the truth. God is presented only as a comforting God. Sin and repentance aren't mentioned. David Wilkerson wondered about the "soft messages" many pastors give with never a mention of the need for repentance. He wondered why. "Are they afraid of losing people? Do they fear being unable to make mortgage payments? Are they mindful of needing people to give more toward the church's growing expenses? I'm convinced these things combine to persuade good men to preach a soft message."[4]

Pastors also compromise the message when Bible passages are loosely interpreted. Pastor Ted distorted Scripture at the beginning of a sermon series on prayer in February 2008 and at the launching of the prayer meeting in April 2008 described in chapter 6. Loose interpretations of Scripture abound in our culture.

**The good shepherd rules his sheep.**

"Encourage and rebuke with all authority" (Titus 2:15). Pastors and teachers hold authority over church members. "Your rod and your staff, they comfort me" (Ps. 23:4). The shepherd's staff sets boundaries for the sheep. Pastors must encourage and rebuke, guide and set limits. Church members must be held accountable and at times be disciplined. This is not easy in today's world. Our culture rejects the idea of bowing to authority. We expect or even demand our "rights." We want to do our own thing, and our culture supports this. Holding members accountable is a difficult but essential task.

**The good shepherd guards his sheep.**

"The good shepherd lays down his life for the sheep. The hired hand is not the shepherd who owns the sheep. So, when he sees the wolf coming, he abandons the sheep and runs away. Then the wolf attacks the flock and scatters it" (John 10:11–12). The good shepherd guards the sheep from predators. The wolf in shepherd's clothing does not. False-teacher pastors have invaded the church—appointed by the theologically liberal hierarchy to naïve churches with weak lay leadership. They mislead the sheep.

Our culture is a predator invading the church by undermining faith, belief, truth, and morals. Cynicism and unbelief reign in the world. The church is compromised by the lure of the world—by money, fame, and power. Materialism and pragmatism are rampant even in the church. Families disintegrate due to divorce or are stressed by over-scheduled life styles and pressure to get ahead. High-tech gadgets, inane TV programming, and violent or X-rated entertainment dull or even pollute our minds. Pastors and church leaders must do all in their power to guard the church from the predators of our culture.

**The good shepherd seeks his sheep.**

"Suppose one of you has a hundred sheep and loses one of them. Does he not leave the ninety-nine in the open country and go after the lost sheep until he finds it?" (Luke 15:4). Many leave their church without saying good-bye as we did. Many stop going to church due to disappointment and hurt over incidents or changes in their church. Do church leaders go after lost sheep who wander away? Not always.

Some pastors appear less than Christ-like toward people who leave church, referring to them disparagingly as "church hoppers." Rick Warren in *The Purpose Driven Church* says that reaching out for potential new members is more effective than contacting leavers. "It usually takes about five times more energy to reactivate a disgruntled or carnal member than it does to win a receptive unbeliever."[5] A sheep that already knows Christ's voice isn't worth going after? Notice the disparagement. Aren't we all carnal? Also, do we do what is effective or what is loving?

Gordon MacDonald, in his fictionalized book *Who Stole My Church?*, describes the painfulness of church members leaving—*from the pastor's point of view*. He writes:

> Speaking as a pastor, you give your heart to the people of a congregation if this work is indeed a calling. You invest in them, think about them constantly, try to find ways to build Christ into their lives. You exult in their spiritual development. You share their difficult moments. And you rejoice when good things happen to them.... If you really do give away your heart, then when people leave, they take a piece of it with them.[6]

I'm sure this is very painful for pastors, but MacDonald fails to see it can be just as painful for leavers. Instead, he questions whether a member who left was truly converted, since he ended a lengthy relationship with his church. The member expresses anger when he leaves. He too, is hurting. He too, has invested his heart in that church, but MacDonald views him negatively. Pastors, please understand the viewpoint and struggle of leaving members. Leaving is as difficult and painful for those leaving as it is for those who are left behind.

Many churches pay a great deal of attention to the assimilation of new members. How much follow-up do they do when members don't show up? When members quit coming to church? Is there an exit committee, a sending forth with blessings and love? Leaders should reach out to missing members; offering to sit down and talk with those who are struggling. Leaders should listen to them, trying to understand their needs, wishes, maturity, or immaturity, all with love.

The Lifeway survey of people who switched churches reported, "The top two reasons for leaving the church are 'the church was not helping me grow spiritually' and 'I did not feel engaged/involved in meaningful work in the church.' These are actually very encouraging findings. The fact that the majority of church switchers express a desire to grow spiritually and become active in service should strike a chord of optimism for leaders."[7]

This study should stir leaders to pursue missing members. Someone should notice when any member leaves. If a family member leaves and fails to communicate, wouldn't we search for that person to find out if he or she is okay, to convey love and care, to let them know they are missed? The good shepherd searches for his lost sheep.

## EXALT GOD

Pastors must exalt God. Pastors must nourish their own relationship with God. Without this, all else is useless. A church can't grow beyond the level of their pastor's faith. Pastors have a difficult job description, but a marvelous Employer. Ministering to the flock is an awesome responsibility and a magnificent purpose. God calls and empowers each pastor to carry out his job description; keeping the flock true to God and his Word.

## Chapter 10

# Worthy Worship
## "Majesty, Worship His Majesty"

Worship is coming into the presence of God and leaving changed.

—Author unknown

God is spirit, and his worshipers must worship him in spirit and in truth.

—John 4:24

RAIN SPLASHES ON the windshield as I drive home in a downpour. The gas gauge reads empty. My spiritual gauge also sits on empty. With fifteen more miles to go, I worry and stew, but keep going. "Lord, help me." *I ran out of gas in my teens and my Dad rescued me.*

"Lord, help me." Suddenly I remember—cars today are different; they have a reserve tank good for twenty-five or thirty miles. My fear vanishes. *Thank you, Lord!* Another thought comes! *I'm a new model, also—a new creation; I have a reserve spiritual tank, a connection to God. He fills and refreshes me when my spirit sags.*

## CAVEAT TO READERS

This chapter required much thought, prayer, and study. The worship issues in today's church are a conundrum. With a humble heart, I present my own viewpoint and understanding about worship. I hope readers from all types of churches will read this prayerfully. I hope the information in this chapter will inspire us all to wait on God more and more, in our daily lives and in our corporate worship. God desires worshippers. He also desires unity in the church. We need to pay attention to what pleases God.

## WORSHIP DEFINED

"They who wait for the Lord shall renew their strength; they shall mount up with wings like eagles; they shall run and not be weary; they shall walk and not faint" (Isa. 40:31 ESV). What a promise! When we wait on God, he strengthens us. Our spirit soars like an eagle. "He gives strength to the weary and increases the power of the weak" (v. 29). Worship is waiting on God. We bow before him. We praise him. We glorify him, and he strengthens us.

Worship lies at the heart of the Christian faith. Moses and the Israelites worshiped God. His presence and glory filled the tabernacle and covered their travel—as a cloud by day and as fire by night (Ex. 13:21). Moses spent days in the presence of God, and his face glowed (Ex. 34:29). Jesus worshiped regularly in the synagogue, taught his disciples to pray, and told the woman at the well to worship "in spirit and in truth" (John 4:24). The New Testament church worshiped together with songs and teachings from Scripture. Paul told the Colossians, "Let the word of Christ dwell in you richly as you teach and admonish one another with all wisdom, and as you sing psalms, hymns and spiritual songs with gratitude in your hearts to God" (Col. 3:16). Paul stressed orderly worship that would teach and enlighten us.

Worship connects us with the presence of God. True worship, opening our hearts to God and praising him, is fearful and astonishing. It changes us. Worship is as vital to our faith as breathing is to our bodies. We bow in adoration, devotion, respect, and awe. God is holy and eternal. We are finite. We humble ourselves in this holy encounter. We meet God weekly in corporate worship as a church body. The fragrant aroma of his presence in us and in the church increases in proportion to our prayer and worship.

This chapter focuses on four aspects of worship: music, prayer, the message, and Communion. Three other dubious changes to worship will also be mentioned.

## MUSIC

"Sing praises to God, sing praises; sing praises to our King, sing praises" (Ps. 47:6). We worship our holy God through music, singing praises together. Music touches our souls and opens our hearts. The music at Main Street Church profoundly affected Mike and me. Prior to returning to church, our life was devoid of music. The well-crafted worship with organ, choir, and corporate hymns filled a deep void, connecting us with God and with our sisters and brothers in Christ. As a child and as a teenager, I enjoyed singing hymns; the words to hymns were embedded in my memory. Mike also remembered hymns from church with his grandparents. Hymns and anthems refreshed our knowledge of the truths of the faith, and inspired our souls.

Since then, Christian music has enriched our lives. In addition to the music in church, we enjoy music by Bill Gaither, Kathy Troccoli, Michael W. Smith, Larry Ford, Sandi Patty, Steve Green, David Phelps, Rich Mullins, the Brooklyn

Tabernacle Choir, Vineyard Music, Revival in Belfast, and contemporary versions of hymns by Selah and Travis Cottrell. We have eclectic tastes in music—at least we thought we did.

**Musical Frustration**

The music at Hillcrest Church morphed from a blended contemporary/traditional mix to very loud music with simple, repetitive lyrics, often about us rather than about God. Earsplitting, dissonant music replaced a joyful time of worship. Worship took on the flavor of entertainment with the focus on the musicians, especially the worship pastor.

Many Christians grapple with frustration and wonder why Christian music is a divisive battleground. Changes in worship, designed to appeal to seekers, reject the hymns and classical music traditionally used in praising God. Most Christians will accept some changes in music when it is harmonious, singable, and theologically sound. The volume, dissonance, and simplistic lyrics do not edify or unite us in worship.

Our culture is saturated with music of questionable quality, with music played extremely loud, and with music that is discordant, sinister, and dark. Should the church adapt to the culture in this way? Aren't we supposed to be different, set apart? We can invite and accept others without adopting their values. Many will need hearing aids at a young age if churches continue to keep the drums and amplifiers turned up. There are valid objections to the loud, discordant contemporary music now played.

Christian journalist Julia Duin, in her book, *Quitting Church*, writes about a visit to Mars Hill Church: "A rock band, Brothers of the Empty Tomb, comprised of young men dressed in black, was blaring as announcements were flashed on a huge screen. Suddenly the music switched to a heavy rock version of 'I'll fly away.' The congregation was supposed to sing, but the band's volume was so loud, it was impossible to hear any voices. Then we swung into 'Testify,' another rock selection, and I glanced around. Hardly anyone *was* singing."[1]

Chuck Colson tells of listening with teeth clenched while his congregation sang praise music until, "One Sunday morning, I cracked. We had been led through endless repetitions of a meaningless ditty called, 'Draw Me Close to You.' The song has zero theological content and could be sung in a nightclub, for that matter. When I thought it was finally and mercifully over, the music leader beamed at us and said in a cheerful voice, 'Let's sing that again, shall we?' 'No!' I shouted loudly.... I am convinced that much of the music being written for the church today reflects an unfortunate trend—slipping across the line from worship to entertainment."[2]

### Hymns and Theology

Songs sung in contemporary services often have little or no theology in the lyrics. In contrast, the great hymns teach the doctrines of the faith. This is true also of well-done contemporary hymns such as "Majesty" by Jack Hayford, "The Blood Will Never Lose Its Power" by Andre Crouch, "Mary Did You Know?" by Mark Lowry, and "Because He Lives" by Bill and Gloria Gaither. Wayne Grudem, in *Systematic Theology*, ends each chapter with the words to a hymn on the subject of the chapter. In picking hymns to relate to the Christian doctrines he "realized that the great hymns of the church throughout history have a doctrinal richness and breath that is still unequaled."[3]

Kevin Twit, a campus minister in Nashville, Tennessee, reports many young people are returning to the old hymns. He tells about a college student who, when exposed to hymns, was overwhelmed. She had not noticed the imagery and poetry in hymns. To her, hymns were boring. Now she's in love with hymns and delights in their wisdom and truth. Hymns have changed her life. With hymns, her worship now centers on God and draws her closer to him. Twit says students all over the country are searching for old hymnals. Interest in hymns has become contagious. They look for profound hymns and develop new music to go with the traditional words.[4] This is great news.

## PRAYER

"My house will be called a house of prayer for all nations" (Isa. 56:7). Traditional worship opens with a brief prayer and closes with a benediction or blessing. Midway in the service a longer intercessory prayer lifts the needs in the church body up to God. Hearts and minds are united before the Father in these moments of supplication. Pastor Wesley's beautiful, pastoral prayers at Main Street Church often brought worshipers to tears, including me. In his prayers he identified with us, helping us face inner pain and give it to God. The pastoral prayer became the high point of the worship service, the "tipping point" in opening hearts to hear God's Word in the pastor's message.

Today's contemporary worship spends little time in prayer. Hillcrest's contemporary service consisted of a half-hour of singing led by the worship pastor, and a half-hour message by the pastor. A short prayer at the beginning and at the end offered token respect to God.

Yet prayer is crucial to every Christian's walk with God. We need prayers of adoration, confession, thanksgiving, and supplication in Sunday worship. We need to pray each kind of prayer. They feed our souls. Spiritually starved Christians weaken the church.

Without this, where do we find corporate prayer? Where and when do Christians learn to pray? Adult Bible classes spend time in prayer but are attended by only the most faithful members. Wednesday night prayer meetings, once held at every church, are now virtually extinct. Grace Church is an exception. Their Wednesday night prayer meeting is small in numbers, but powerful, because it is largely spent in intercessory prayer.

Terry Teykl, in *The Presence Based Church*, questions whether contemporary churches are seeking God's presence and sees this as our greatest need. He says: "People are thirsty for the living water, a personal encounter with a living God, and no degree of human involvement or techno-gospel production can satisfy their souls. The consumer-based church is a mirage that promises refreshment, but delivers an empty cup. Only the Presence of God can quench their thirst and fill them."[5] We need to seek God's face and spend time listening and praising him. Our churches must be spiritual filling stations.

## Communion

> The Lord Jesus, on the night he was betrayed, took bread, and when he had given thanks, he broke it and said, "This is my body, which is for you; do this in remembrance of me." In the same way, after supper he took the cup, saying, "This cup is the new covenant in my blood; do this, whenever you drink it, in remembrance of me." For whenever you eat this bread and drink this cup, you proclaim the Lord's death until he comes. Therefore, whoever eats the bread or drinks the cup of the Lord in an unworthy manner will be guilty of sinning against the body and blood of the Lord.
>
> —1 Cor. 11:23–27

Holy Communion is a crucial sacrament or ordinance of the church providing a "sacred moment" to remember Christ died for us. All Christian churches observe Communion.

Most of them do so once a month, though it may be called the Eucharist or the Lord's Supper. It is a special service remembering that Christ died on the cross for us. When we take Communion, we act out the final moments surrounding Christ's sacrifice. The bread is a symbol of Christ's body. The wine represents his blood. Jesus himself told us, "Do this in remembrance of me" (Luke 22:19). Communion is a meaningful ritual which touches us and changes us, because it reminds us of the price God paid to redeem us. Communion is a means of grace in which we are strengthened and spiritually nourished for the journey of faith and service to our Lord.

The Walk to Emmaus deepened my understanding and appreciation of Communion. We took Communion daily in silent reverence, emphasizing the holiness of Communion. Coming forward and kneeling for Communion under Pastor Jim at Main Street involved body and soul; there were no passive participants. Jim heightened the experience by pressing the bread into our hands, reminding us of the nails in Christ's hands.

Communion at Hillcrest was extremely brief. The one-hour worship service included a half hour of music and a half-hour message—so something had to give on Communion Sunday. Due to the speed in serving Communion and the limited explanation of the meaning of it, some friends facetiously referred to it as "McEucharist"—a drive-through experience. On at least one occasion, Communion was served in an unworthy manner. At Grace Church, Communion is deliberate and meaningful, with varied biblical comments from the pastor about the significance of taking the bread and the cup.

Julia Duin describes Communion at three well-known emerging or emergent churches. At Mars Hill Church she expected to hear the Communion Scripture read, but didn't. People rushed to receive Communion from casually dressed ushers who held baskets of bread and chalices of grape juice or wine. At Cedar Ridge Community Church, Communion was brief with a short comment about the sacrament of Communion and a liturgy from the Episcopal service. Individually they took Communion and visited a sort of religious buffet at locations around the church for prayer, lighting a candle or giving an offering. At Imago Dei Community Church in Portland, Oregon, loud music played during Communion and there was no explanation of it.[6] "Whoever eats the bread or drinks the cup of the Lord in an unworthy manner will be guilty of sinning against the body and blood of the Lord" (1 Cor. 11:27).

Is Communion being served in a worthy manner today?

### The Message

"The word of God is living and active. Sharper than any double-edged sword, it penetrates even to dividing soul and spirit, joints and marrow; it judges the thoughts and attitudes of the heart" (Heb. 4:12). The sermon or message is the central ingredient of a worship service. Over the last twenty years, we have heard one thousand sermons! The majority of them pointed us to Christ, and were true to his Word. We need to understand how all Scripture points to Christ. We need to hear the Word and be taught its meaning and significance.

Theologians David Wells and Charles Swindoll both lament the lightweight topical messages popular today. Swindoll in his book *The Church Awakening* says "God's Word has been replaced with artificial food.... No solid food is served, only junk food. Everyone leaves hungry." He goes on to say, "One of the most devastating causes of erosion in the church has been the drift of pastors from the bold proclamation of God's Word. Many who step into pulpits today do so reluctantly, sometimes even apologetically. It's as if they are ashamed of their calling.

The ground of conviction has slipped from beneath their feet. As a result, their congregations remain famished."[7]

David Wells in his book, *The Courage to be Protestant*, says, "Unless the congregation is being confronted—is being informed by the truth of God's Word—it will leave as empty and confused as when it came in, no matter how good it may feel about itself. Unless the congregation is learning to think God's thoughts after him in this world, one that is highly modernized and postmodern in its ethos, it will not be able to function with a Christian worldview."[8]

Do we need one type of sermon for seekers and another type for believers? Does one kind of message reach the lost and another kind disciple the saved? Mark Driscoll doesn't believe so. He says both seekers and believers need to turn away from sin and accept Jesus in order to have the Spirit's power in their life. He believes one message can reach both groups.[9] Hopefully, many churches of all varieties realize the truth in this and won't compromise the message of Scripture. When the Word is watered down, taken out of context, or when difficult parts are omitted, the church is malnourished. We need to hear and know the whole Truth.

Joshua Harris in his book, *Stop Dating the Church*, emphasizes the importance of listening to the message. He says the value of the message has to do with hearing the Word of God. This is what impacts us, rather than the excellence or status of the minister. God speaks to us through preaching from his Word. For this reason we need to be attentive listeners.[10] Scripture supports this. "Faith comes from hearing the message, and the message is heard through the word of Christ" (Rom. 10:17). Good listeners take in the message, and it feeds their souls.

## OTHER CHANGES TO WORSHIP

Three other dubious changes to worship are the omission of silence, light, and tradition. These have been an integral part of worship in the past. Do we really want to delete them?

### Silence

"Be still, and know that I am God" (Ps. 46:10). Silence is anathema to our culture. We are saturated with noise. We need silence in order to slow down and breathe. We need at least brief silence during worship to face our sins and wait for the presence of God. Matt Redman, well-known worship leader and author, says: "The God of glory, who thunders over the mighty waters, reveals Himself intimately and quietly to the depths of our heart. When alone and when gathered as a worship community, we must learn to listen for Him—in the sound of sheer silence."[11]

Contemporary worship today offers virtually no silence. A church-consulting firm advised videotaping the church service and playing it back, side-by-side with MTV. The more similarity, the more likely the service will reach people under age forty. They recommended silence longer than five seconds should be eliminated.[12] What about, "Be still, and know that I am God?" (Ps. 46:10). What about listening in *sheer silence? Listen* has the same letters in it as *silent*.

In contrast to the purposeful avoidance of silence in most contemporary worship, Timothy Keller's church (packed with young adults) intentionally includes silence—a full minute of silent prayer to praise God. Keller says this time of holy silence surprises or even shocks people, waking them up to take worship seriously; enabling them to experience the presence of God.[13]

## Light

"God is light; in him there is no darkness at all" (1 John 1:5). God "lives in unapproachable light" (1 Tim. 6:16). We need light. A lack of light affects our bodies' circadian rhythms, causes seasonal affective disorder (SAD), jet lag, and sleep deprivation. We need sunlight to meet our need for vitamin D. Light enhances our health.

God is light, but many worship him in the dark. Many contemporary churches have built or purchased warehouse-type buildings and created sanctuaries resembling movie theaters. The dark, windowless walls allow easy viewing of song lyrics and videos illustrating the message. These churches worship in the dark, week in and week out. Hillcrest Church dramatically altered worship by changing a light and airy sanctuary, a sanctuary with many windows, to one as dark as night.

Rick Warren, in *The Purpose Driven Church,* writes about sanctuary lighting: "Lighting has a profound effect on people's moods. Inadequate lighting dampens the spirit of a service.... Most churches are far too dark.... Even churches with plenty of windows often cover them up.... I believe that church buildings should be bright and full of light.... If you want to wake up your services, brighten up your environment. Take the curtains off your windows. Throw open the windows and doors. Turn on all the lights."[14]

Jesus is the Light of the world. Let's worship him in the light.

## History and Traditions

"You must teach what is in accord with sound doctrine" (Titus 2:1). We have an historic faith with two thousand years of tradition. God came into our world—into our time and space dimension, to reveal himself to us. The creeds and confessions that express our faith must be taught to new generations. Instead, the move to contemporary services has led to a "dumbing down" of our faith, omitting the call to worship, responsive reading, Scripture, deliberate time for prayer, and biblical benedictions. These edify and involve the congregation and point our attention Godward. These losses are major. And the changes don't "win" the lost. Instead they frustrate the worship of the "found."

Christmas carols, traditional Easter hymns, and Easter Scripture were deleted from Hillcrest Church's worship in 2007 and 2008. Christmas celebrations and Holy Week services are significant markers and link even unbelievers to their childhood church connections. More importantly, these teach us the crucial meaning of the incarnation of Jesus Christ, his work on the cross, and his resurrection. The carols, hymns and Scripture from both these holidays are in our deep memories, even in our spirits. They touch us and bring us close to God. Why would a church change or omit these?

## United in Worship

Worship as a church should involve and include everyone. Churches must prayerfully balance appeal to young adults and seekers with the needs of mature believers. All Christians need to participate in singing, confessing sin, praying for others, praising God, hearing the Word, and taking Communion. Worship is not a passive experience, nor is it entertainment. Worship should be counter to our culture.

We can approach God in many ways, in many styles of worship. What matters is that we open our hearts to him and surrender to his will. We need to worship with our church family and be in prayer as we go about our daily routines. Our Sunday worship is fed by daily prayers and vice versa. We need to live with the awareness we are in Christ, and he is in us. This is the way to transformation.

CHAPTER 11

# CHRIST-LIKE MAKEOVERS

## "TRUST AND OBEY"

The church exists for no other purpose but to draw men into Christ, to make them little Christs.

—C. S. Lewis

Rid yourselves of all malice and all deceit, hypocrisy, envy, and slander of every kind. Like newborn babies, crave pure spiritual milk, so that by it you may grow up in your salvation, now that you have tasted that the Lord is good.

—1 Peter 2:1–3

AS A PREACHER'S kid, I attended Sunday school and church every Sunday of the year, every year. I received perfect attendance pins for eleven years, with each pin fastened to the one above it, forming a chain. I proudly displayed the chain on the lapel of my coat and wore it to church and school. It now rests in my jewelry box. In Sunday school we memorized verses and received stars for this accomplishment. Did this make a difference? Here's a journal excerpt:

**May 16, 1990**

> An eerie thing happened. I've been comparing myself to the prodigal son. One night I spotted several New Testaments on a top bookshelf. I climbed on a chair to reach them and opened the first one gingerly. Awe and wonder flooded my soul. I read in my father's handwriting "To Dorothy J. Clark, for memorizing Luke 15." The date and name of the church were written below. Luke 15 is the story of the prodigal son!

Memorizing Scripture didn't stop me from drifting, but it helped bring me back to the church. Today, few children go to both Sunday school and church. Family lifestyles are too busy to commit two hours or more on a Sunday morning. Children who do go to Sunday school are rarely expected to memorize. Though I drifted away from church, I credit my childhood knowledge of Scripture and the words to hymns as instrumental in drawing me back.

The term "casual Christian" should be an oxymoron. This chapter is about the elements necessary for taking the "casual" out of Christians; the factors that are essential for building up and transforming the church. The four elements are discipling, growing, healing, and holding accountable.

## Discipling

"All Scripture is God-breathed and is useful for teaching, rebuking, correcting and training in righteousness" (2 Tim. 3:16). Church members must be taught the great truths of the faith. We must understand the Word of God in its entirety. As children, we should cut our teeth on Scripture. Many Christians are biblically challenged or biblically illiterate. Many know a smattering of the Bible but don't have an overview of the amazing scope and consistency of Scripture. Only the most faithful members of mainline churches attend a Sunday adult Bible class or a Bible study during the week. The majority are untaught except by what they glean from the Sunday sermon. The Bible stories we learn as children are not enough to make us strong Christians.

How can we be discipled? Bible study is essential, and many excellent studies are available. Three outstanding books that give an overview of the Bible are: *What the Bible Is All About* by Henrietta Mears, *Learn the Bible in 24 Hours* by Chuck Missler, and *Halley's Bible Handbook*. A fourth book, *How to Read the Bible for All It's Worth* by Gordon Fee and Douglas K. Stuart, teaches how to study the Bible. These books offer a wealth of information. In addition to learning on our own, study in a group keeps us learning in a planned way.

*Disciple Bible Study*, with weekly two-and-a-half-hour meetings and daily homework, is offered by some Methodist churches. *Disciple* participants read 80 percent of the Bible, studying the themes the first year. Many at Main Street Church completed all four years of *Disciple Bible Study* and continued in other studies. *Bible Study Fellowship* is another excellent in-depth Bible study. Kay Arthur's *Precepts* teaches a valuable verse-by-verse Bible-study method. Beth Moore, Maxie Dunham, and Henry Blackaby also offer excellent studies.

Another effective way to disciple members is through retreats, camps, and conferences. The *Walk to Emmaus* is a life-changing four-day short course in Christianity available to adult Christians of any age or denomination. (This is a Methodist version of *Cursillo*). Many of us came to Christ or deepened our walk with Christ in our teens and twenties due to retreats or Christian camps. These are the reason for our strong faith today. Christian conferences for adults can have a similar effect at any age.

Small groups can be life-changing. They nurture commitment to faith, deepen friendships, and support accountability. Following the *Emmaus* weekend, weekly "Share Groups" are formed with members asking each other accountability questions. Mike and I were in weekly *Emmaus* share groups for a number of years. Mike's group continues to meet for breakfast and sharing once a month. A faithful women's group met at my home for years. Each week we shared our closest moment to Christ and our plans for spirituality, study, and action. This format took our conversation to a deep level, and prayer knit us together and strengthened our walk with Christ.

Hillcrest Church promotes short-term study groups with the entire congregation studying the same material. These coincide with a sermon series and are a good way to reinforce and unify teaching. Grace Church encourages members to join ongoing small groups for fellowship, study, and prayer.

*Alpha* is another excellent tool available for discipling members and even non-believers. *Alpha* answers questions about the Christian faith such as: Why did Jesus die? How does God guide us? Why and how do I pray? Small groups discuss these questions after a video lecture on each subject. The groups are encouraged to continue beyond the end of *Alpha*.

We took *Alpha* at Hillcrest Church in 2005, and our diverse group continues, with new members joining and some dropping out. Our diversity is intergenerational, with members from age thirty to eighty. In the six years together, we have been through many video-based studies. We also have shared in the birth of six babies to four couples, prayed for and sent letters to one member in jail and a son in jail, supported and prayed for a member with prostate cancer and a woman with a serious blood-clot problem, plus we have shared prayer requests weekly about many less serious issues. As a group we participated in several Hillcrest Church outreach events, we celebrated three wedding anniversaries at once (fiftieth, thirtieth· and twenty-fifth), had many potluck dinners, showers for new babies, and we observed Communion together at Easter. We have become family.

## GROWING

"Confess your sins to each other and pray for each other so that you may be healed" (James 5:16). Growing requires awareness of our mistakes, flaws, and sins. This awareness can happen in the discipling experiences described above. It must happen in order to become mature Christians. But sin is a word neglected in the modern and postmodern church.

What is sin? "All have sinned and fall short of the glory of God" (Rom. 3:23). All have sinned. Let that sink in. We're full of pride; we're self-centered rather than being God-centered. We aren't open and authentic; we're not humble and vulnerable. We deny our flaws, our emptiness, our lies, and our manipulations. We want to appear good or even perfect.

Awareness of my sin hit me when we returned to church. I knew I had sinned in drifting away from Christ—rejecting him, after knowing him in my youth. Recognition of my sin unfolded further in a twelve-step study at Main Street Church. Deep repentance swept over me with step four, "a searching and fearless moral inventory." I wrote thirty letters asking forgiveness and making amends where I could. I read the letters to Mike and to Wesley and delivered them in person or by mail to those I'd offended. This was scary and life-changing. Celebrate Recovery is another Christian twelve-step program helpful in facing our sin and growing up. In a ladies Bible study at Hillcrest, Lynn, the teacher, suggested we journal Psalm 51 (about David's sin) one verse a day through the forty days of Lent. I did this, prayerfully applying each verse to myself. God revealed previously undiscovered sins, buried like forgotten pets at an old address. This type of exercise is needed by all Christians. At the beginning of every worship service, Grace Church offers a silent time to repent of sin. Repentance comes first before we can truly worship, though it too is an act of worship.

True prayer with open hearts before a holy God brings us to repentance. Confession of sin and repentance go together and result in changes in our behavior. Otherwise our faith is counterfeit, and grace is cheap. All Christians need to repent on a regular basis, even daily. I suspect few of us do so. Few churches today focus on sin and the need to repent, even though the Lord's Prayer includes, "Forgive us our sins, for we also forgive everyone who sins against us" (Luke 11:4). The whole idea of sin goes against the grain of our feel-good, do-as-you-please society.

The secular world looks on people as good. The Christian faith says we are basically bad or sinful, even depraved. The church must help us face our sin and help us repent. Without repentance, we will be stuck. Without repentance our growth as Christians becomes as dead as the Dead Sea. The Spirit can't flow through us to minister to others. A caterpillar must die to his life as a caterpillar and be born again as a butterfly. We also must die to our old life and be born again.

## HEALING

"He heals the brokenhearted and binds up their wounds" (Ps. 147:3). Many Christians need healing. We live in a fallen world and bring to church all the problems we experience in the world. No one escapes this life without struggles. Some problems are obvious—major illness, loss of a loved one, and loss of jobs. Other struggles are hidden—marital problems, alcoholism, drug addiction, financial difficulty, depression, mental illness, and stress. Ministries to heal hurting or immature believers are essential and life-giving. This is CPR for the church.

Some churches have a care pastor trained in Christian counseling. Pastors who are good listeners, accepting of differences, and not easily shocked can be very helpful to their congregation. Wesley's counseling certainly impacted my life. Pastors do need to know when it's best to refer, and they need to know their own limits time-wise as well as emotionally.

Stephen Ministers provide valuable help to those suffering a loss, facing illness, dealing with separation or divorce, and other life crises. These lay caregivers are carefully trained in communication skills—especially listening. Stephen Ministers are supervised monthly, and confidentiality is respected. Hillcrest Church has a very active and excellently managed group of Stephen Ministers.

Educational groups also help people heal and grow. Equipping Ministries International offers low-cost weekend seminars in communication skills with biblical application to various issues of life today. Seminars include Listening for Heaven's Sake, Speaking the Truth in Love, Renewing the Mind, Breaking Free from the Past, and Embracing God's Grace. Mike and I found these very helpful for our marriage and our spiritual growth. We've referred many others to these seminars with similar positive results.

Mike and I witnessed more change in marriages in the Third Option than in most counseling, and couples continued in the program longer. How could this be? The low cost—simply a donation—is a factor in the length of involvement, but this doesn't explain the dramatic changes. Counseling focuses on problems, while the Third Option focuses on solutions. In counseling, couples are adept at rehashing their issues over and over. The Third Option teaches individuals they can change only themselves—not their partner—and they learn tools for change. When one person changes, this changes the dysfunctional pattern. Group members also give couples a reality check—every marriage has problems. Couples learn to understand and appreciate their differences. Sharing couples tell their story, including how Christ helped heal their marriage. This demonstrates that even the worst problems can be overcome. We witnessed radical, lasting changes. There were also instances when counseling and the Third Option worked well together.

Another excellent approach to helping marriages is a Weekend to Remember. Other resources can be found at www.smartmarriages.com. Christians need to be determined to resolve their marital differences and remain together. The health of the church depends on this.

Celebrate Recovery, a Christian version of the twelve steps of AA, is helpful for people who are addicted or codependent. Christian programs for facing financial problems such as Financial Peace University, and Good $ense Ministry are also available. Some churches offer practical help to the unemployed—with resume preparation, networking, and interviewing. Resolving our personal issues strengthens the body of Christ.

### HOLDING ACCOUNTABLE

"Anyone who listens to the word but does not do what it says is like a man who looks at his face in the mirror and, after looking at himself, goes away and immediately forgets what he looks like" (James 1:23). The church has forsaken its job of holding members accountable. Christians divorce as frequently as non-believers. Sexual sins abound in our culture and are rampant in the church. Divorce is excused by our culture and by many churches. We can accept people without condoning the ending of a marriage.

Most couples, even Christian couples, spend more time and thought planning their wedding than planning their marriage.

Premarital counseling, required by most churches, can prevent divorce when the significance of the marriage ceremony and the biblical basis for making a lifelong commitment is emphasized.

A premarital program, PREPARE, helps couple understand the seriousness of marriage. PREPARE is used at the counseling center at Main Street Church and by many pastors. Each individual fills out a questionnaire. These are scored by computer, matching the results. The counselor/pastor uses this information to help the couple see their strengths—areas in which their marriage will likely flourish, and their growth needs—areas where they may have problems. This counseling helps each couple think through specific future issues.

Hillcrest Church offers a mentoring program for engaged couples. Each couple is paired with a mature couple and meets with them through their first year of marriage. At Main Street Church couples separated and divorced secretly, even though the Third Option was widely advertised and met at the church year round. Embarrassment and pride stand in the way of seeking help, especially from the home church and pastor. Many churches are now aware of the enormous need to strengthen marriages. They are offering marriage programs and holding couples to their vows.

Grace Church's detailed, biblical marriage policy holds couples accountable; reconciliation is encouraged in virtually every situation. As a counselor, I agree, having experienced the sad and devastating ramifications of divorce in the lives of many couples I counseled and in my extended family. I weep over the families split apart by divorce. I weep because the marriage vows are demeaned in our culture. The church must lead the way in holding Christian couples accountable to God's Word and to their vows. The Bible says so.

The moral standards of the culture are lax at best. Do Christians live more ethically than unbelievers? Do we need accountability in other areas—envy, gossip, lying, pride? Are white lies okay? Is gossip "normal" and to be ignored by pastors and elders? Are church members held accountable for their spiritual practices and growth?

Accountability is evident in other groups. Rotary dismisses members who have three unexcused absences in a row or who attend less than 60 percent of the weekly meetings. Bible Study Fellowship enforces similar rules. Wouldn't it be interesting if churches had an attendance and participation requirement! Scripture supports this, "Let us not give up meeting together" (Heb. 10:25).

Some churches do hold members accountable. Jim Cymbala, pastor of the Brooklyn Tabernacle in New York City, said this to new members:

> I charge you, as pastor of this church, that if you ever hear another member speak an unkind word of criticism or slander against anyone—myself, another pastor, an usher, a choir member, or anyone else—you have authority to stop that person midsentence and say, "Excuse me—Who hurt you? Who ignored you? Who slighted you? Was it Pastor Cymbala? Let's go to his office right now. He will get down on his knees and apologize to you, and then we'll pray together, so God can restore peace to this body. But we will not let you talk critically about people who are not present to defend themselves."
>
> New members, please understand that I am entirely serious about this. I want you to help resolve this kind of thing immediately. And meanwhile, know this: If you are ever the one doing the loose talking, we will confront you.[1]

Cymbala says nothing else as easily destroys churches as gossip and slander.

John MacArthur learned a church member's husband left her to live with another woman. He called the husband and said, "I'm calling in the name of Christ for you to move out of that woman's place before you sin against God, your wife, and your church." The man was shocked and went back to his wife. He thanked MacArthur and said, "I didn't want to be there. I was tempted and thought no one would care."[2]

Joshua Harris in his book, *Stop Dating the Church,* suggests we look for and join a church that would be willing to kick us out! He says, "I gain a wonderful sense of protection in knowing that if I committed a scandalous sin and showed no repentance, my church wouldn't put up with it. They would plead with me to change. They would patiently confront me with God's Word. And eventually, if I refused to change, they would lovingly kick me out. Remember that the purpose behind church discipline is first to restore."[3]

## Accountable to Love Each Other

Accountability involves the "one anothers" of Scripture. These are scriptural instructions about how we are to treat each other in the church as well as how we are to treat unbelievers. Here are a few of them:

> Be devoted to one another (Rom. 12:10).
> Love one another (Rom. 13:8; 1 Peter 1:22).
> Spur one another on (Heb. 10:24).
> Encourage one another (Heb. 3:13; 10:25).
> Accept one another (Rom. 15:7).
> Teach and admonish one another (Col. 3:16).
> Serve one another in love (Gal. 5:13).
> Be kind to one another (Eph. 4:32).
> Forgive each other (Eph. 4:32).

What would the church look like if we practiced these instructions? The most important one is the last one, forgive one another. Unforgiveness hurts us, and it hurts the church. A healthy church loves. A loving Christian is humble and vulnerable.

## SPIRITUAL WARFARE

"Resist the devil, and he will flee from you" (James 4:7). Christians need a clear understanding of what the Bible says about our fallen world. We must understand the battle we face. "Our struggle is not against flesh and blood, but against the rulers, against the authorities, against the powers of this dark world and against the spiritual forces of evil in the heavenly realms" (Eph. 6:12). We need to put on the full armor of Christ daily before going out into the world (Eph. 6:13–17). How many Christians know and use this armor?

I learned about spiritual warfare in a charismatic prayer group, and this boosted the consistency of my faith. This learning confirmed experiences as a counselor in which I encountered a few people who were deluded by the devil, if not in league with him. Spiritual warfare is real.

Neil Anderson, in *Extreme Church Makeover*, asks "How are we going to help people reach their full maturity in Christ if they have no idea how to overcome the evil one? The unfortunate truth is that many Christians, including leaders, have seemingly uncontrollable appetites and behaviors. The sin-confess-sin-confess-and-sin-again cycle does not deal with all of reality. It should be sin, confess, repent, and resist."[4]

Whom do we resist? James says, If you resist the devil he will flee from you (James 4:7). He'll run away! If we put on the armor of God mentally each morning, pray daily, and walk in his light, we will overcome Satan and our flesh. Neil Anderson's books help individuals resolve anger and hurt by understanding they are new creations in Christ. This is medicine to defeat the devil. Anderson's book *Who I Am in Christ* increased my faith and deepened my walk.

## CORPORATE BONDAGE

There are no perfect churches, but some are more dysfunctional, disturbed, or "dis-eased" than others. Church members bring baggage—resentment, unforgiveness, and sin. Pastors and leaders carry baggage after painful church experiences. When there's historic baggage from any source, it's difficult for a church to have unity or freedom in Christ. How can the local church be renewed? Many churches need help. They are troubled and dysfunctional.

Anderson says, "If the [church] leadership lacks an adequate theology of resolution, they either lower their standards and expectations or live in denial and continue to muddle along with business as usual.... Individual freedom must come to the leadership before organizational freedom can be accomplished. The church Body cannot rise above its leadership."[5]

This rings true. As a family counselor I could see that the parents' maturity determined the progress of the family. *Extreme Church Makeover* describes a method church leaders can use to free themselves and their congregations from corporate bondage. I highly recommend it. We need healthy, united churches.

When the church disciples, grows, heals, and holds accountable its members, the church is transformed. Then we have a story to tell to the nations!

CHAPTER 12

# GO AND TELL, GO AND HELP

## "WE'VE A STORY TO TELL TO THE NATIONS"

"Do you know about the sin of the desert?" "No," we replied, wondering.
"The sin of the desert is knowing where to find water and not telling others."

—Our Jewish guide in Israel, 1999

Go and make disciples of all nations, baptizing them in the name of the Father and of the Son and of the Holy Spirit, and teaching them to obey everything I have commanded you.

—Matthew 28:19

**Christmas Day, 1990**

DON'T BRING THAT kitten in here," I snapped.

"It's fifteen degrees outside," Scott replied. My son, visiting from California, seemed shocked that I would object. His eyes pleaded with me. I glanced at the gray ball of fur, thin and injured. Mixed emotions swirled inside me. *She is cute*, I thought.

"I guess she'll die if we don't let her inside." My irritation dismayed me. *Why didn't I want to accept this poor, wounded creature?* Instead, I risked alienating my irreligious son. It was Christmas, but my peace on earth had vanished with a cat's whisker.

*Does Matthew 25 apply to kittens?* I wondered. "I was hungry and you gave me something to eat, I was thirsty and you gave me something to drink, I was a stranger and you invited me in" (v. 35). I thought of another Christmas when there was no room in the inn. It amazed me that this kitten appeared on Christmas Day. *Did God send her?*

The next day Scott took the kitten to the vet. She needed surgery to close a deep gash in her side. Scott paid the vet bill and bought food and kitty litter. "I was sick and you looked after me" (v. 36). My irreligious son showed more compassion than I did. "Whatever you did for one of the least of these … you did for me" (v. 40). I have a long way to go in living my faith.

## Our Service to Christ

Jesus commands us to love our neighbor—feed the hungry, clothe those in need, visit the sick and those in prison (v. 35–36). He also commands us to go into all the world and make disciples (Matt. 28:19). The first is outreach and social action, the second is evangelism and missions. Though these are different, they overlap; they can and often do go together. We witness/tell the good news in the context of helping those in need.

I'm more compassionate now than I was on Christmas Day, 1990. Our service to Christ and to others grows from our relationship with him. It's the result of our salvation; it's the fruit of knowing him. The kingdom was prepared for us *from the foundation of the world* (Matt. 25:34 ESV). Our salvation is a gift; it's unmerited and not something we have earned by our good deeds. Our good deeds follow our salvation. As we grow in our relationship with Christ, we die to self and give of ourselves more and more.

Evangelism and outreach can be done for the wrong reasons. Church members pressured to "go and do" feel guilty if they don't go, or proud if they do. Members already involved in outreach don't need the repetitive message. The strong emphasis on outreach at Hillcrest Church resulted in the neglect of messages on growing in our relationship with Christ. This is crucial, because our service flows from our worship. For this reason, worship is the first priority of the church, not evangelism.

John Piper puts it this way, "Mission is not the ultimate goal of the church. Worship is. Mission exists because worship doesn't. Worship is ultimate, not missions, because God is ultimate, not man. When this age is over and the countless millions of redeemed fall on their faces before the throne of God, missions will be no more. It's a temporary necessity. But worship abides forever."[1]

### FULFILLING THE GREAT COMMISSION

Many Christians focus on social action or political change and assume they are fulfilling the Great Commission. They aren't. We are commanded to be compassionate and generous toward others, especially the poor and oppressed. However, when we concentrate on these needs to the neglect of our call to share the gospel with others, we miss the point of Christ's sacrifice.

Mark Dever says, "When our eyes fall from God to humanity, it's not surprising that social ills replace sin in our concerns. Today, horizontal problems—problems between people—often obscure the fundamental vertical problem between us and God."[2] We are commanded by Jesus to tell others where the Living Water can be found, but we can't share this Water without first knowing the Source.

Part one of the chapter details our experiences in missions and outreach. We are sinners on the way to becoming more

Christ-like, not experts or models. We hope our story will inform and inspire others. The second part of the chapter explores witnessing in today's world with its vast mixture of belief and unbelief.

## Missions and Outreach

In my teens and early twenties, I thought God was calling me to be a missionary. The American Baptist mission board rejected me, but I landed a job as girls' director at a Baptist community center in downtown Washington, D.C.—my mission field for two years. Then I moved on to social-work graduate school where I drifted away from God and church.

During our secular humanist years, Mike and I were oblivious to and/or judgmental about evangelism and outreach by Christian churches. When we returned to church, the light dawned. Our eyes were opened. We then realized Christians founded many, many agencies and organizations that help the poor and the needy. In spite of our social-work knowledge and careers, we didn't appreciate, until then, that Christians founded the YMCA, the YWCA, hospitals, universities, the Salvation Army, the Red Cross, and many other social agencies. We also didn't appreciate the many missionaries who spent their lives spreading the gospel around the world. Now, the stories of missionaries such as David Livingstone, E. Stanley Jones, Frank Laubach, Jim Elliot, and Don Richardson amaze us. We're also in awe of evangelists Billy Graham, Franklin Graham, and others who spend their lives telling the good news of Jesus Christ.

### Main Street Church Missions and Outreach

Main Street Church encouraged members to give money to many national causes such as *One Great Hour of Sharing*. Individually, members participated in Christian outreach organizations, and other charities. And we gave gifts to needy families at Christmas.

When I applied the *twelve steps* to my life in 1992, I asked God to forgive me for not helping care for my parents during their last years on earth. To make amends, I offered to visit an elderly woman in the congregation. I was paired with a crotchety, retired teacher, angry with the world. Though a stroke crippled her body, and her vision had dimmed, her mind remained sharp. For more than four years I visited, I listened, I attempted to encourage and affirm her, and I felt a sense of loss when she died. We had become friends. She blessed me in spite of her attitude.

In 1995 Main Street Church decided to use endowment funds to open a Christian counseling center. Due to our mental-health expertise, Mike and I were chosen to co-chair a committee to study and later set up Grace Christian Counseling Center. In the midst of this, a newspaper article about the Third Option caught my eye. I felt God nudging me to start a group at the Center. I argued with God, "Lord, this is beyond me. I'm an introvert. I don't like groups." However, ultimately I told him yes. The Third Option and Grace Christian Counseling Center opened in 1996 and drew clients from all over the area. Mike and I spent many hours leading these ministries. Each of these projects stretched me, taking me out of my comfort zone. Helping marriages was our mission field for eleven years, leading the Third Option group at Main Street and at Hillcrest.

Pastor Jim encouraged Main Street Church members to reach out in new ways. We invited neighbors to church with door-to-door evangelism for a special weekend program. He arranged vacation Bible school with our Salvation Army neighbor, and involved us locally in *Crop Walk* for feeding the hungry. Under Jim's leadership we took Communion to shut-ins four times a year using the same elements served to the congregation earlier in the day. At Christmas we went caroling to shut-ins and rang bells for the Salvation Army. A sister Methodist church, in a poor area of the city, closed and reopened as a ministry to Hispanics. Many of us participated in outreach to this ministry. For many years we organized a Christmas shop for needy families. Mothers came and picked out new toys for their children. We helped wrap the gifts, served refreshments, and gave a short program—connecting with them and sharing the gospel. These were new and meaningful experiences for Mike and me.

In the summer of 1999 Jim led us on a home-mission trip. We put on a vacation Bible school at a small rural church, built a wheelchair ramp for a crippled man, and painted the interior of a community center. These experiences bonded the team members and pushed us out of our comfort zones, surrendering to Christ in new ways.

One afternoon the kitchen team (including me), driving to the church to prepare dinner, bumped the fourth of five cars in a bumper-to-bumper accident. We comforted an elderly woman, who was shocked and distressed by the accident. Her car had to be towed. She didn't want her husband called because of his heart condition, so Mike came to the rescue and took her home. We were stuck there for three hours while the police interviewed each person, measured the road, and wrote reports.

During the wait I kept asking God, "We're on a mission trip, why did we have an accident?" I knew we helped the elderly woman. I later thought about the peacefulness of the accident scene. The other drivers and passengers remained calm and friendly while rearranging their plans and waiting endlessly. In today's world this is remarkable. I think God used us as witnesses in talking individually with the police and with others as we waited. We are salt and light to bystanders in the midst of life's accidents. We don't know when Christ in us is visible to others or when he uses us. And we had pizza delivered for our dinner that night.

**Hillcrest Church Missions and Outreach**

Hillcrest Church majors in outreach and missions to the tune of 18 percent of their budget. The church contributes to an African-American sister church, a homeless shelter, and Habitat for Humanity. Hillcrest also supports an ongoing ministry collecting used books for missionaries.

Once a year Hillcrest Church organized a huge outreach. Teams of people helped around the city in a variety of ways. One year our small group mulched shrubs and weeded flowers at an elementary school. Another year we painted a park gazebo. Occasionally, Hillcrest Church held a free car wash to demonstrate Christ's love in a tangible way. Many people went on short-term mission trips to Haiti, Dominican Republic, Mexico, and Nicaragua. Many members volunteered as mentors to at-risk children and with many other parachurch organizations. It is an outreach-minded church.

**Grace Church Missions and Outreach**

Grace Church supports over forty missionaries and six missions and outreach organizations, locally and in other countries. They planted and support a church locally, one in Bulgaria and one in India. Short-term mission teams visit the foreign church plants to assist in their ministries with more than just money. The young people go on short-term mission trips yearly to a local camp for underprivileged children, and to the Cherokee Indians in North Carolina. Grace Church is also a regional center for Franklin Graham's Shoe Box ministry.

Mike and I are surrounded by missionaries at Grace Church. A number of retired and local missionaries are members, and we often have visits from missionaries. A mission conference every year with speakers, small-group sessions, and many missionaries describing their ministries, informs the members of the work being done. We pray for these missionaries regularly and receive frequent e-mails describing prayer needs and praises. Grace Church knows their missionaries. Knowing missionaries personally makes a difference. These are real people in real-life situations, spreading the gospel. Support for missions is budgeted separately, but amounts to 20 percent of the combined budgets.

Most churches have a benevolence fund. This fund is used to help people in emergencies, such as paying utility bills they can't manage. All churches visit sick or shut in members of the church. Too often, only the clergy do the visiting, which places a burden on them. At Grace Church, the deacons assist the pastors and elders with the care needs of members and put on a monthly lunch for the seniors. In all three churches small groups take care of their members with meals and visits in time of need. This works well with choir members rallying around a choir member and Bible class members helping out class members.

**Prayer While Writing This Chapter**

> Lord, forgive my provincialism. I have grown up so privileged and so isolated from the needs of the world and so ignorant about the utter poverty, the hopelessness, the ravages of war, and the unfairness of life for so many, many people. I've been writing the chapter on evangelism and having trouble with what to say—writing to justify my denial of the need, and my not doing more, writing to brag (?) about what I have done to help others. Forgive me, Lord.
>
> The current *PrayerPoint* by Samaritan's Purse, picturing poor, war-ravaged, and sick people made me weep for so much of humanity, as well as be amazed at what you are doing through Franklin Graham and this ministry. Open

my eyes, Lord. Forgive my self-focus, near sightedness, and arrogance. Humble me before you and show me your will now in my life. How can I make a difference and share your gospel around the world? Use me, Lord.

## WITNESSING IN TODAY'S WORLD

"Always be prepared to give an answer to everyone who asks you to give the reason for the hope that you have. But do this with gentleness and respect" (1 Peter 3:15). God used two comments from others to draw us back to him. In 1989, while viewing the church before our son's wedding, his future mother-in-law referred to God in a hushed voice. With surprise I thought, *She really believes in God.* Six months later, a friend said, "My church is like an extended family." This attracted me. Both of these women witnessed without realizing it. What we say to others matters. A casual comment about our faith can make a life-changing difference. Many of our friends never mentioned their faith during our years away from God. We didn't know many even went to church. Christians are called to be witnesses.

### Learn How to Witness

To witness effectively we need to understand the faith or lack of faith of friends and acquaintances. Our children and grandchildren need to recognize and comprehend the vast differences in other faiths, so they will stand firm in Christ. Teenagers face a whole new world in college. Many of the students and professors they meet will be unbelievers—atheists, agnostics, and secular humanists. In our culture, non-Christian beliefs are often mixed with Christian beliefs. This blending of beliefs is pervasive and subtle. It's called syncretism. The faith of Christian college students will be challenged by the unbelief of the culture. Knowledge can protect them from the lure of syncretism and will help them be witnesses. Young and old alike need some basic understanding about other religions. The world is smaller now. We will meet Muslims, Buddhists, Hindus, as well as Jews, atheists, and agnostics. We will also meet Jehovah's Witnesses, Mormons, pantheists, Wiccans, and Unitarians. If you don't think you'll meet anyone with these beliefs, think again. A number of my relatives, raised in Christian homes, now include self-proclaimed Buddhists, pantheists, Wiccans, atheists, agnostics, and Unitarians. If you don't meet other faiths in your own family, you will at work or in your neighborhood. Here's a brief primer to get us started. My knowledge is new, but growing, and I intend to learn more.

## Comparison of World Religions and New Religious Movements

### Buddhism

Buddhists believe the purpose of life is to escape from the wheel of suffering through self-denial and detachment from the world. This usually takes more than one lifetime. Karma, or destiny, depends on behavior in this and in previous lives. Nirvana, or enlightenment, is attained by losing your individuality and merging with the non-personal spiritual force. Buddhists don't believe in a god.

### Hinduism

Hindus believe in non-personal gods and goddesses, thousands of them. Hinduism says everyone is a god. An afterlife is a series of reincarnations dependent on their good behavior in each life, leading to becoming one with god. The material world is an illusion. Individuality is called "maya," which means illusion. We are part of god.

**Islam**

Muslims believe in one god, Allah, and Mohammed was his prophet. God is not a personal being. Muslims must recite the Qur'an over and over in the original Arabic, not violate many taboos, and do the will of Allah perfectly. Their faith is expressed in rituals.

**Judaism**

Jews believe in one God, who is the maker of all things. They believe the messiah has not come yet. Conservative and Orthodox Jews attempt to keep strict Sabbath laws, food laws, and holy days.

**Mormons and Jehovah's Witnesses**

Mormons and Jehovah's Witnesses both deny the deity of Christ, believe in a new revelation, deny the sole authority of Scripture, and deny that salvation is by grace alone. Both are cults. Both are authoritarian, chauvinistic, dogmatic, legalistic, and intolerant of others. Mormonism originated in 1830 when Joseph Smith "became a god." Smith taught that from Pentecost to 1830, all believers were wrong. None were Christian. Jehovah's Witnesses began in 1879. Jehovah is not the God of the Bible. The trinity is viewed as a satanic doctrine. Jehovah's Witnesses believe they earn heaven.

**Scientology**

Scientology is a cult based on the writings of L. Ron Hubbard. Beliefs are a mishmash of Judeo-Christian monotheism, Hindu polytheism, and pantheism. Mankind is caught in a cycle of reincarnations.

**Unity**

Unity claims to believe in the divinity of Jesus, but says we are all children of God and share the divine potential. God is understood as spiritual energy, everywhere present, and available to all people. Salvation is found in conscious understanding of one's innate divinity and putting this knowledge into practice in everyday life.

**Unitarian-Universalists**

Unitarian-Universalists reject the Christian doctrine of the Trinity and the divinity of Christ. They stress reason and individual conscience.

**Pantheism**

Pantheists believe that god and the material world are one and the same. God is present in everything. We are all part of a non-personal spiritual essence.

**Wicca**

Wiccans are involved in nature worship (pantheism) and witchcraft. Wiccans worship a deity that is both male and female, a mother goddess and a father god, who created all that exists. They believe they have divine power. They can tap into the power and energy of the spirit world by casting spells.

**Atheists and Agnostics**

Atheists believe there is no god, no creator. Agnostics aren't sure there is a god. Both value reason and science and are skeptical about belief and faith. They are secular humanists valuing autonomy, individualism, with no absolutes, no right or wrong.

## SORTING IT OUT

Don't let the list of religions and cults overwhelm you. Here's an easy way to sort it out. Christianity is different from all other faiths in two ways:

1. Christianity is the only faith with belief in a personal God. There is a vast difference between belief in Jesus and belief in a vague non-personal force.
2. Christianity is the only faith that doesn't require works. All other faiths require keeping laws, performing rituals, doing "works"—do, do, do. Christians are saved by grace. We receive unmerited favor.

## SYNCRETISM

The mission field in this country is enormous. Many people did not grow up in church, are not interested in church, and know little about the Christian faith. Many claim they are spiritual, but attend no church. We are living in a culture of syncretism where beliefs are combined as one chooses. Two examples follow:

A sitcom on television shows a family planning a baby dedication. The father wants the baby baptized, but the mother desires a Hindu ceremony. The grandparents arrive and insist the baby should be circumcised by a Jewish rabbi. A family argument ensues. In the end, they compromise and say, "Each of us will bring our own religious leader and we will do all of them."[3]

Here's another example of syncretism from Don Bartel:

> One of our neighbors is a very well-educated woman who believes she is a reincarnated thirteenth-century artist and a more recently reincarnated American Indian. She takes yoga classes from a Buddhist monk. In line with reincarnation,

> she believes in Hinduism. She is an unpublished author and writes about the American Southwest. Her religious philosophy of choice is Indian mysticism. Nevertheless, she attends an Anglo-Catholic church because she likes tradition and structure. She likes to talk with me about the Bible. She believes it would be great if we could have a five-way dialogue with an Indian chief, a Buddhist monk, a Hindu priest, a Catholic priest, and me. As you can see, she is very eclectic in her religious outlook. Even when she talks about Christianity, she is not talking from a biblical point of view. She is typical of many around the country.[4]

These examples sound like some of my relatives. I have intentionally reached out by e-mail to my nieces and nephews, dialoguing about their beliefs with several of them for varying periods of time. This deepened my understanding of their diverse viewpoints in the world. One relative accused me of proselytizing. Uncertain how to respond, a chapter in *Telling the Truth* advised me to admit my motives were mixed and included a wish to convert.[5] I wrote back:

> My motives for dialoging with you are complex and no doubt include some wish to convert you. I also want the best for you—a successful and happy life. I respect and love you as an adult member of my family and want to know you better and understand your worldview. Our conversations have enriched me, and I hope they will continue.

Our dialoging hasn't continued beyond this, but hopefully seeds were planted. (I continue to reach out occasionally with family news.) It's important while witnessing to be honest. God wins souls, anyway, not us.

Our culture insists on "political correctness" and claims all faiths are equally valid. If it works for you, it's okay with me. The culture claims all roads lead to God. Yet the beliefs of each faith differ, and each faith requires different things from believers. Christians are saved by faith alone. All other faiths say you must do, do, do in order to reach heaven or "nirvana."

Christianity is the only faith in which God comes down to us. Christianity is the only faith in which God paid the price for our salvation. Christianity is the only faith with belief in a personal God, teaching love, humility, and service. Contradictory beliefs can't both be true. Notice beliefs of others that are contradictory to the Christian faith. This can open the door to witnessing. We can share and defend our faith rationally, yet with love and respect.

## SENSITIVE WITNESSING

Dan Kimball in his book, *They Like Jesus but Not the Church*, emphasizes the need to form friendships first, listen to what others believe, understand what attracts them to their "faith," and be respectful. We know this, but don't always practice it. Only when we do these things should we attempt to explain the Christian faith. Kimball has interesting visuals in his book—a historical map of when each faith began, and pictures of three different mountains to God showing why all roads don't lead to God. He says various faiths have similar teachings at the base of the mountain, but they each climb a different mountain leading to a different God.[6]

Another way to create a receptive environment is described by Susan Hecht:

> If someone is sitting in a dark room and you flip a switch that floods the room with light, the person in the room will undoubtedly wince and turn away from the source of light with eyes shut tightly. If, on the other hand, you walk into the dark room with a candle or flashlight, the person in the darkness will be attracted to the light. Sometimes we take a

> floodlight approach to evangelism. We understand that God is light and that in him there is no darkness. We feel that we must share everything immediately with the unbeliever. If the person winces and turns away, we conclude they are not ready and we move on to someone else.[7]

We must be sensitive when we share the good news with others. We can light a candle; not a blinding spotlight. We can be gentle and loving; yet also bold.

## Prayer for Missions

Missions, evangelism, and outreach must be bathed in prayer. Missionaries need prayer support. Our world needs prayer. Prayer makes a difference. If all Christians prayed specifically for missionaries around the world and for the needs in every country, we might have revival! This daunting task of praying for the entire world is made easier by a marvelous book, *Operation World,* by Jason Mandryk.[8] The book gives detailed demographics of every nation in the world, lists answers to prayer, and challenges for prayer. Dates at the bottom of the page make it easy to read this book devotionally throughout the year, praying for each country. Published in 2010, the information is reliable and up to date. Grace Bible Church is using it in prayer meetings. Reading *Operation World* increases our knowledge of other countries and cultures and is guaranteed to lessen our provincialism.

> Dear Father,
>
> We have decided to follow you. We will go wherever you send us. We offer our gifts, our talents, and our time to you. Help us listen and know when you want to use us to meet particular needs. Increase our desire to give, serve, and help others. We can't meet every need, but we can meet some needs, through your enabling power at work in us.

We thank you for the work you've given us to do thus far. The work has helped us!

Give us the desire to support your missionaries throughout the world. We hope to play a part in bringing someone to you. We have witnessed about you. We've also missed opportunities to witness. Forgive us, Lord. Help us boldly declare, Jesus is the way, the truth and the life! Help us hold to your teachings as we face our changing culture and changing churches.

## Chapter 13

# Changing Churches in a Changing Culture

## "O God, Our Help in Ages Past"

> Sweeping in from the cultural sea, a mountainous wave of change threatens to wash the church away. It's a postmodern flood of mind-boggling techno-culture, problems your grandparents couldn't have imagined, and religious pluralism that embraces everything except spiritual absolutes.
>
> —Leonard Sweet

> So then, brothers, stand firm and hold to the teachings we passed on to you, whether by word of mouth or by letter.
>
> —2 Thessalonians 2:15

A STRANGER CAME to live with us years ago at the invitation of my parents. I didn't question his place in our family. In my young mind he had a special niche. My parents were intelligent, upright people and good to me. Mom taught me right from wrong and Dad taught me to obey, but the stranger told stories. He kept us spellbound for hours on end with brilliant adventures, spooky mysteries, and hilarious comedies. The stranger made me laugh and cry.

He never stopped talking, but Dad didn't seem to mind. Dad ruled our household with certain moral convictions, but the stranger never felt obligated to honor them. Our longtime visitor even got away with four-letter words. He talked freely about sex. He got by with blatant, suggestive, and embarrassing comments. Time after time, he opposed the values of my parents, but they never asked him to leave—and he's still there. His name? We just call him TV. And he has a wife now. We call her Computer.

Technology invaded the home when TV came on the scene, and it changed the family dramatically. In many homes there is little silence, less conversation, and almost no time for family games or activities. TV rules family life and has lowered our ethical standards. Technology has changed the home.

Technology invaded the church and changed it dramatically. Like TV in the home, technology in the church entertains and teaches us with visual images and stories. Technology has benefits—offering visual and audio means to spread the gospel. It also has drawbacks—diluting the message of the church or adapting it to secular culture. Technology has changed the church.

Leonard Sweet says an immense "wave of change threatens to wash the church away."[1] This chapter describes changes in the church and changes in our culture we must understand to avoid being swept away. It's crucial for Christians to learn about and pray about:

- The influence mega-churches have exerted on virtually all churches.
- The effect of culture's "isms"—narcissism, pragmatism, and relativism—on the church.
- The direction of the postmodern church, the emerging church, and the emergent church.

Books have been written on each of these subjects, so I will only give thumbnail sketches from my own experience and reading. I urge readers to learn more by reading some of the books in my endnotes.

## MEGACHURCHES

Megachurches, or seeker-friendly churches, are conservative Protestant churches with two thousand or more people attending worship each week. Compared to traditional churches, the dress code in megachurches is casual, the attenders are younger, and worship is contemporary. Megachurches are usually located in heavily populated suburban areas. They own a large expanse of land and are near an expressway. Often a senior pastor with charisma has built the church in a decade or so from a few members. The staffs of these churches often include many full-time ministers in addition to the senior pastor. Megachurches offer a wide variety of social, recreational, support, and outreach programs.

Traditional Protestant churches have fifty to five hundred members, worship is more formal and dress less casual. The majority of churches in the United States are small, with one hundred members or fewer.

Megachurches appeared on the scene in the last thirty years or so. A recent Associated Press article with the headline, *Megachurch attendance skews younger*, cited a study done in 2008 which surveyed nearly twenty-five thousand people who attend twelve megachurches. The highlights reported were:

- The average age of megachurch attenders is forty, compared to nearly fifty-three at a typical Protestant church. Nearly two-thirds of megachurch attenders are under forty-five, double the numbers in Protestant

congregations of all sizes. The vast majority are between eighteen and forty-four.
- Nearly a third of megachurch attenders are single, compared to 10 percent in a typical Protestant church. They also tend to be wealthier and better educated.
- Megachurch-goers volunteer less and give less money than other churchgoers.[2]

We attended a Vineyard megachurch several times at the invitation of friends. This church built an enormous new building in the nineties and gave their smaller building to an African-American congregation. Their mission is to show God's love in a practical way through acts of kindness. They certainly live their mission.

The Vineyard churches have pioneered new ways of being a church. Other well-known megachurches are Rick Warren's Saddleback Church in Lake Forest, California, and Willow Creek Community Church near Chicago. These and other megachurches attract many unbelievers and seekers with contemporary music, casual dress, and a focus on giving to their community. They bring many seekers to Christ and are change agents in their communities with innovative outreach ministries. Though their worship is often held in a dark theatre-like auditorium, the Holy Spirit still speaks to hearts there.

We remember one particular Spirit-filled service at the Vineyard in October 2007. We delighted in the praise music, and laughed out loud at an impromptu skit of Paul's Damascus Road experience. Following this, the pastor articulated the Vineyard's goal to facilitate the kind of transformation Paul experienced. While driving around one day, he came to the town of Pansy and discovered the Pansy Church. He thought about this and concluded too many churches are pansy churches. He is tired of sissy churches with little transformation—churches made up mostly of casual Christians.

Megachurches are bold and energetic, unlike sissy churches. They have broken the "churchy" mold with the change to contemporary music, use of technology, and many weekend services to accommodate busy lifestyles. Megachurches have awakened many traditional churches dominated by casual Christians going through the motions of faith. Megachurches have led the way to change.

But has church membership grown? Are there fewer casual Christians and more committed Christians? Michael Horton, theologian and author, questions the success of seeker churches in reaching and winning more people to Christ. Horton says, "Although the church growth (or seeker-driven) movement defends its perpetual innovations as more missional, there has been no growth in the rate of professed conversions during this period. In fact, there has been decline."[3]

Willow Creek Community Church has been in the vanguard of megachurches with multiple services at six sites and an attendance of twenty-three thousand per weekend. A survey done by Willow Creek, covering members at six churches including Willow, surprised the leaders. It showed a great deal of dissatisfaction by mature believers. An editorial in *Christianity Today* said, "The study shows that while Willow has been successfully meeting the spiritual needs of those who describe themselves as 'exploring Christianity' or 'growing in Christ,' it has been less successful at doing so with those who self-report as being 'close to Christ' or 'Christ-centered.' In fact, one-fourth of the last two groups say that they are either 'stalled' in their spiritual growth and/or 'dissatisfied' with the church."[4]

*One fourth* of the Christians who are mature in their faith said they are not growing or are dissatisfied with their church. This is huge. Yet Willow replied that these Christians expected too much from the church. According to Willow, mature Christians must find their own way to grow—but Scripture says we are "to be built up in the church" (Eph. 4:12–16). We should take some responsibility for our own growth, but discipling, even of mature believers, must be centered in the church. We are all works in progress. Left to our own devices, we may stumble. The megachurches as well as many mainline churches emphasize outreach at the expense of Bible study and evangelism. The church should do all three.

### MEGACHURCH INFLUENCE

Leonard Sweet says "It makes me nauseatingly sick that half a dozen megachurches in USAmerica cast the molds for what goes on in the majority of Christian churches around the world. It's not their fault. It's ours."[5]

This bothers me also. Lured by technology and marketing strategies, virtually every church has launched a contemporary worship service. At Main Street Church, Jim initiated a contemporary service in the sanctuary, holding it at 8:00 AM prior to the Sunday school hour. A core of thirty attended this inspiring worship. Some of these attended the 10:30 service also. I suspect the Methodist hierarchy mandated a contemporary service, hoping to bring new and younger members to the church. This hasn't happened at Main Street Church—the average age is still fifty-five to sixty. Instead, the church is now divided with about forty-five members attending each service, and membership has declined.

At Hillcrest Church, the shared wisdom from the megachurches claimed the more services a church held, the larger the attendance. Contemporary worship would draw twenty-to-forty-year-olds and achieve their goal of increased attendance and younger demographics. Loud rock music replaced the beautiful blended worship as previously described. Membership declined, and demographics remained the same—average age is still forty-five to fifty.

Churches with two types of services divide Christians by worship style and often by age. Shouldn't the church be heterogeneous? The church needs to create worship that teaches, inspires, and ministers to all. Jesus prayed for our unity.

### UNIQUE CHURCH NICHE

When the mission of a new church is to attract young unbelievers and young seekers, it's consistent to choose Christian music that will draw them, as long as the lyrics are about God (not about us) and have some theological depth. My concern is with established churches forty or fifty years old or more that disregard the faithful senior members of their congregations and switch to Christian rock music in the hope of attracting twenty-to-thirty-year-olds. My concern is with smaller mainline churches copying megachurches or new church plants rather than prayerfully developing their own unique worship niche. When we attempt to copy each other, we become like clones, without heart or soul. "Eminent domain" decisions are pragmatic, not prayerful, and can destroy rather than transform the church.

There are many churches within fifteen minutes of our home, and the majority of them hold contemporary services at the ten-to-twelve-o'clock hours on Sunday morning, catering to seekers and copying each other. Why don't some churches focus on being traditional, yet vital, as Timothy Keller has done in New York City? His flourishing church offers a very traditional worship service (described in chapter 10). A friend of mine who visited Keller's church says he focuses on God's truth and has a gift for teaching deep theological truths in an understandable way. The church will grow in depth when more pastors exhort the church to reason biblically as Timothy Keller does. Churches that blend hymns with contemporary music promote unity; they offer a worship service to touch all hearts.

There are niches available. Some churches could reach out to unbelievers or unchurched seekers who are in their forties, fifties, and beyond. Many over forty are single, divorced, or hurting. This mission field is wide open, and they need the gospel just as much as the youth. Christian leaders must prayerfully think outside the box to make their church a unique church, meeting unique needs as God leads them. One size does not fit all. God loves variety.

In developing a niche, a church must choose which avenues not to pursue. Peter Scazzero, in his book *The Emotionally Healthy Church*, says, "It takes great maturity for a church to identify opportunities and to choose not to take advantage of them. Each church, like each small group, ministry, and individual, has God-given limits. How many services should we have on Sunday? What about a Saturday night service? Others are doing it successfully and growing. If we are two hundred people, why not become four hundred or eight hundred, or ten thousand? I always assumed continued numerical growth for every local church was God's will. It is not."[6]

Mark Driscoll puts it this way, "Pursuing potential rather than calling gets a church off mission. Too many churches try to do too much. This is because their mission is too big, or they accommodate too many people in the church who have their own various missions. A local church needs to prayerfully and carefully define what God has called it to be and do and then excel at that."[7]

Church leaders, please let God lead you; let God give you a vision for your church. What kind of church is God calling your church to be? Don't make changes until you know this. Then make changes gradually, keeping the unity of the congregation in mind. Deliberate and detailed communication about possible changes and respect for all viewpoints will help a congregation accept changes. Loving, prayerful actions transform the church.

## Marketing the Church

Consumerism and materialism have invaded the church. Church marketing caused a problem at Willow. Their weekend worship services were geared to seekers with little or no depth. The marketing at Hillcrest Church (mentioned in chapter 5) included redecorating the entire children's area with Disney-type murals in the halls and classrooms. The gym, previously used for basketball, as well as church breakfasts and dinners, was remodeled with glitzy carpet, a stage, and computer games. This is now devoted to high-energy worship for grade-school children. Three large screens and computer games were added in the teen room as well. Another facet of Hillcrest's marketing was dropping the word Baptist from their name, believing many seekers would not come into a church with that label.

All of the above changes grew out of the corporate model Hillcrest and many other churches have adopted. The church, organized and run as a business, is pragmatic and glitzy rather than prayerful and caring. Hillcrest hired key staff members based on their dynamic personality and let go faithful staff members who "weren't dynamic." A business model is used in the organization of many churches, though the teaching may be faithful to the Word. This seems schizophrenic to me. A church operating with a corporate model of pragmatism is not modeling the message it is presenting. This quenches the Spirit and aborts transformation.

## Valuing Seniors

What place do seniors have in churches today? Are they marginalized or valued? Are they seen as requiring much care and being too old to do the work of the church? Or are they a precious resource? Stuart Briscoe, well-known pastor and speaker, says seniors are the closest to eternity, but they are ignored or isolated in our youth-oriented churches. Many seniors are in need of care and attention. Many elderly are lonely and isolated. Many don't know Christ and are nearing the end of their life. The church needs a vision for reaching and serving this large and growing population.

Senior members also have much to contribute to a church, Briscoe says. Their wisdom, skills, and experience are a valuable resource. He believes seniors who are alive are not finished in the purposes of God. Briscoe encourages churches to do more than plan trips and meals for seniors, though these are valuable for their social needs.

He recommends seniors start or join prayer groups in their church. Seniors have time to pray and know how to be still. As intercessors they can have a powerful impact on the church. Briscoe also suggests seniors reach out to the lonely and unbelieving elderly. The seniors in his church have reached out to every nursing home in their area developing relationships.[8]

I would take it a step further and suggest seniors can do anything God calls them to do. But they need to be encouraged in this and included in the possibilities. At Main Street Church, the leaders of the Disciple Bible Studies and those heading up the Hispanic outreach are seniors. At Hillcrest Church, the Christian book ministry for missionaries is headed and manned largely by seniors. At Grace Church, many seniors have gone on mission trips, including a woman in her seventies who went to Mongolia on a ten-day educational mission in 2008 and in 2010. At each of our churches the seniors carried out a great deal of the outreach as well as teaching classes and serving in leadership.

A church that includes and values all ages, from birth to death, from one day old to one hundred years old, has a beauty and dimension of life missing in postmodern churches with their youthful demographics. We need children and youth in our churches so we can teach the good news to the younger generation and so this new generation can and will lead the church into the future. But we also need the wisdom, vision, and perspective of the elderly.

## CULTURAL CHANGES: NARCISSISM, PRAGMATISM, AND RELATIVISM

A secular worldview has infiltrated the church like a virus infecting the hard drive of a computer. Three related philosophies, rampant in our culture, have seeped into the church like sludge from a broken sump pump. We are awash in narcissism, pragmatism, and relativism.

### Narcissism of our time

Narcissism means self-love or vanity. We can see it in our own self-centeredness, egotism, and self-absorption. We are the center of our world. *Christianity Today* reported on *Time* magazine's person of the year for 2006. The cover of the magazine was a mirror. The person of the year was YOU! The article said:

> Behold YOU. Yourself. You can do it. You did it. Be all you can be. YouTube™. You are the star. It is a proclamation of pure, absolute narcissism. The world ends at my face. Me. My space. My autonomy. I rule my world.
>
> Perhaps the deepest moral challenge to the United States, not only for this year but for years to come, is the ethical form of radical narcissism. This is the condition when human judgment cannot see beyond its own exercise of freedom and exercises that freedom in isolation from "the other."[9]

Chuck Colson tells about a woman named Sheila interviewed by sociologist Robert Bella. "I believe in God," she said. "I can't remember the last time I went to church. But my faith has carried me a long way. It's 'sheilaism.' Just my own little voice." Sheila, as many others today, believes she is her own god. There is no higher power or authority and therefore no need for commitment beyond self. Church groups with this philosophy are knit together only on emotion and their own self interest.[10]

The narcissism of our culture is so extreme that many only think in terms of their "rights" and wants. The thought of serving others, of "dying to self," is alien—not something they want to hear or think about. Compromise, cooperation, and consensus are also alien concepts in our narcissistic culture.

**Pragmatism**

Pragmatism cares only about results. The end justifies the means. We set a goal and go for it. We use common sense and forget idealism. The culture and the postmodern church have become more and more pragmatic in recent decades. The end, the goal to be reached, justifies any means to get there. If technology and bright lights bring more people to the church, spending money on this is justified. Another example came in the mail—a large, slick postcard advertising a church. On the front in bold letters it said, "Church Sucks.... or at least, we thought so." The church that sent this decided the goal of reaching people who disliked church justified using offensive language. Scripture doesn't tell us to do what works—it tells us we are sinners and need a savior.

**Relativism**

Relativism claims there are no standards, no universal ethics, nothing is absolute. There are no objective truths. Right and wrong varies from one culture to another and from one individual to another. You choose your "truth" and I choose my "truth." Nothing is inherently right or inherently wrong.

This belief system has made its way into many public schools and is rampant at universities. Nancy Pearcey gives an example of a dilemma used in a class.

> Students were required to imagine they were planning to murder their best friend. What alternatives could they come up with for accomplishing that goal? Some students were appalled, objecting that they would not choose any methods because murder is wrong. Period. But that answer was not acceptable. The teacher required students to leave behind their preexisting moral convictions, by mentally rehearsing behavior they held to be wrong. The goal of such activities is to detach students from the moral teachings absorbed from outside, so that they will get in touch with their own personal, authentic values.[11]

Yes, our school children are at risk of being taught to throw away all values, beliefs, or ethics. The church also is at risk. A church that is not rooted in the Bible will embrace the relativism of our culture.

## WORLD'S VIEW AND CHRISTIAN VIEW COMPARED

Christians must be aware and beware of the difference between a biblical worldview and the secular worldview of our culture. The difference between the two is like night and day. They are diametrically opposed. Chuck Colson in his book, *The Body*, compares the world's view with that of Christians:

- The world's view is shaped by relativism; the Christian's view is formed out of the objective, revealed truth of Scripture. It rests on absolutes.

- The world's view is secular; the Christian's view is eternal. What we do now is not passing and unimportant; it counts forever.
- The world's view is anti-historical; the Christian's view acknowledges the historical account of God's work from the beginning. History is treasured and respected.
- The world's view is naturalistic; the Christian's view is based on the *super*natural.
- The world's view is pragmatic—do what works; the Christian's view is idealistic—do what is right by objective standards.[12]

How do these views play out in our churches today? Sad to say, the world's philosophies have invaded the church. Christians need to recognize when a church dilutes or distorts the message of the gospel. One example of this given by Horton is the prosperity gospel presented by Joel Osteen, well-known television pastor. According to Osteen, if you follow certain rules or principals you can ask for what you want and prosperity will be yours. This is a narcissistically focused faith based on self improvement.

Another example is Brian McLaren, a leader of the Emergent Village who emphasizes improving the world by conquering problems such as AIDS, poverty, and global warming. His focus is on peace and justice. The teaching of both of these men claim it's up to us to bring about our salvation. Christ is a model to be followed, not our Savior.[13]

## POSTMODERN CHURCHES

The emerging church and the emergent church are the names of postmodern churches, confusing in their similarity. There are thousands of emerging/emergent churches in our country in many denominations. Emergent churches are very liberal and are aligned with an organization named Emergent Village.

Driscoll prefers to call postmodern churches "missional churches" to make it clear they differ from the emergent church.[14] The primary goal of missional churches is to reach out and engage postmodern generations—those in their twenties and thirties who generally are not in church.

**The Emergent Church**

The emergent church minimizes or rejects the core beliefs of the faith. It embraces inclusiveness, spirituality, and making the world a better place. It teaches a "feel good" Christianity. The postmodern era—from 2000 on, is an age of skepticism. Postmoderns believe there is no truth. Truth is whatever you define it to be. There are no absolutes. Language can't convey meaning because it has different meanings for different people at different times. These beliefs (or unbeliefs) are prevalent in our culture and also in the emergent church. History is not factual, because of the biased viewpoint of the writers. Even the history in the Bible is doubted by some postmodern Christians.

Kevin DeYoung and Ted Kluck in their book, *Why We're Not Emergent*, helped me understand the focus of the emergent church and its denial of crucial doctrines of the faith. DeYoung says:

> The main problem in the universe, according to many emergent writers, seems to be human suffering and brokenness. Make no mistake, suffering and brokenness are a result of the fall, but the main problem that needs to be dealt with is human sin and rebellion. Where sin is the main problem we need a crucified Substitute. Where pain and brokenness are the main problems, we need to

> learn to love ourselves. God is no longer a holy God angry with sin, who, in His great mercy, sent His Son to die on our behalf so that divine justice might be satisfied. God becomes a vulnerable lover who opens himself up to hurt and rejection in order to be with us because we are worth dying for.[15]

Emergent church teaching affirms the goodness of humanity and dismisses our sin nature. It offers help for brokenness rather than redemption through Christ's death on the cross. This is secular humanist "feel good" spirituality claiming to be Christian.

**House Churches**

To complicate things further, many missional/emerging church leaders are planting house churches—informal gatherings in homes or coffee shops or elsewhere. They often lack a leader and have no Bible teaching or preaching. They meet for discussions, singing, and the sacraments. They encourage participation by every person, led by the Holy Spirit. Meetings are unplanned and spontaneous. Some live communally and reach out to others, attempting to model the way Jesus lived. Mark Driscoll expresses concern about people getting together to do something spiritual and calling it a church when it's not rooted in biblical doctrine. Jesus is viewed as a good example of living a moral life and the idea of redemption or salvation are missing. "The result is that some emerging churches are nothing short of a complete redefinition of what constitutes a Christian church."[16]

Using Driscoll's and DeYoung's information, I created the chart on the next page to clarify the differences between the emerging churches and the emergent church. I hope this clears up the confusion. The two groups have many similarities and there are exceptions. It's clear that not all postmodern churches are questioning the truth of Scripture. Some are faithful to traditional evangelical beliefs and purposes. This is good news.

**Missional Churches**

| *Emerging Churches* | *Emergent Churches* |
|---|---|
| Evangelical | Diverse Christian traditions, evangelical and Catholic |
| Authority of Scripture | Theological revisionism, denying objective truth |
| Salvation by grace—faith in Christ | No statement of faith, as it limits dialogue |
| Socially and politically diverse | Liberal interests and causes |
| Predominately white suburban | Predominately white urban |
| Social activism/concern for urban poor | Social activism/concern for urban poor |
| Multi-sensory worship | Multi-sensory worship/some contemplative/liturgical |

Evangelical House Churches

## CASUAL CHRISTIANS OR CAPTIVE CHRISTIANS

George Barna in his book, *The Seven Faith Tribes*, defines the seven tribes as Casual Christians, Captive Christians, Mormons, Jews, Pantheists, Muslims, and Skeptics. The Casual Christians represent 66 percent of the adult population of the United States. The percentage of the adult population represented by the other half-dozen tribes includes 16 percent who are Captive Christians, 2 percent Jews, 2 percent Mormons, 2 percent Pantheists, .5 percent Muslims, and 11 percent Skeptics. Barna defines the Casual Christian tribe as "comprised of significant proportions of minimally active born again Christians and moderately active, but theologically nominal Christians." And he says, "If a catalyst were added to this mix to deepen this tribe's integration of faith and lifestyle, or even to simply create a more extensive sense of community and purpose within the tribe, unprecedented changes could occur." Here's a summary of Barna's definitions of casual Christians and captive Christians:

> Casual Christians are driven by a desire for a pleasant and peaceful existence. Captive Christians are focused on upholding the absolute moral and spiritual truths they glean from the Bible.... The lives of Captive Christians are defined by their faith; their worldview is built around their core spiritual beliefs and resultant values. Casual Christians are defined by the desire to please God, family, and other people while extracting as much enjoyment and comfort from the world as possible.... Casuals are about moderation in all things while Captives are about extreme devotion to their God regardless of the worldly consequences.[17]

I consider myself a Captive Christian, but as I read Barna's definition, I'm not so sure. I live comfortably and relish a peaceful life. I don't like confrontation. Moderation is so much easier. I must pray about this, and I hope you will also. Have we surrendered all to him? In summary, Christians, we need to "stand firm and hold to the teachings passed on" to us (2 Thess. 2:15). The wave of cultural change will not destroy the church if we stand firm. When the church is built on the rock of Christ Jesus, nothing will prevail against it. We must become Captive Christians. We must make *Casual Christian* an oxymoron. Read on for the good news of the church built on the Rock.

# Chapter 14

# Transforming Churches
## "The Church's One Foundation"

> The heaviest obligation lying upon the Christian Church today is to purify and elevate her concept of God until it is once more worthy of Him—and of her.
>
> —A.W. Tozer

> On this rock I will build my church, and the gates of hell shall not prevail against it.
>
> —Matthew 16:18 (ESV)

A CRYSTAL CLEAR pool of water dazzles my eyes. Blue skies and puffy white clouds float above. Snowcapped mountains surround the scene; the water mirrors the mountains. I drink in the beauty, take a breath, and dive in. I go down, down, down—twenty to thirty feet … 'til I touch bottom. Clear, deep water surrounds me; it's beautiful, warm.

I'm suddenly fearful … *Can I hold my breath long enough?* … *Can I reach the surface?* … Slowly, I begin rising … I glide upward … The blue skies and the mountains shimmer before me; relief and joy flood my heart … *I did it! I'm cleansed, free, released—I'm transformed.*

This vivid dream lingered with me. The images, symbolic of baptism, dying to self and being raised in Christ—death and resurrection, replayed in my mind. Coming up was the scary part in the dream—not going down. Why would this be? … I pondered it … Oh, coming up out of the water is like a birth, being born again. Coming out of my cocoon is scary. Coming out of my comfort zone requires dying to my old life. It's new, strange, and exhilarating territory. I come up to new life where I can fly like a butterfly, breathe the breath of God, and swim in his Water of Life. I'm a new creation in Christ (2 Cor. 5:17).

## Leaving our Cocoons

A meteorologist discovered that a butterfly flapping its wings in South America changes our weather.[1] Transformation is quietly powerful. We need to change; we need to be transformed. The church, built on the Rock of Jesus Christ, should transform us from caterpillars to butterflies. We need to emerge from our cocoons of safety and sameness. As born-again butterflies, we continue to grow. We feed on the nectar of the Word. We are willing to face suffering, even endure being pinned as specimens to the wall of persecution for our faith.

## Changed by Church

Before my return to church in 1990, my life resembled a black-and-white silent movie with few actors. Now my life is a Technicolor production with beautiful scenery, inspiring music, and many special friends. Music fills my heart and soul, and God's presence brightens each day. As a church member, I am no longer alone. I am part of the fellowship of Christ—a loving support group. Life has meaning and purpose. What greater cause can there be than doing the will of God and being part of his church? Christians are a devout community of people sharing the most significant and magnificent purpose on earth; glorifying God, worshipping him, and spreading the good news of the gospel of Jesus Christ. How thrilling!

I love the church. The church mothered me and fathered me in the best sense of those words. The church taught me the most wonderful truths there are and introduced me to the One who is Truth. The church has been God's instrument to change me.

The church is the most successful experiment in community the world has known. In Sunday school as a child, I sang, "Red and yellow, black and white, all are precious in his sight." We loved this song, even though the church was very white! The church needs more racial diversity, and this is coming in many churches, including our three churches described here. The church at its best accepts all people—rich and poor, sick and well, young and old, sinner and saint. There is no generation gap and no status gap. This is true diversity. Membership in a diverse community where you are loved, accepted, and held accountable is rare in our culture.

## Hurt by Church

Some churches are not change-agents for Christ. Some churches are dysfunctional, disobedient, disheveled, or dead. Many people have been seriously harmed by church. This is a sad fact. I hope those hurt by church will not give up on it, but will seek another church and will seek help and healing for the harm done. Though many have been hurt by the church, many more have been healed and transformed by it. The local church is the only place on this earth where Truth reigns, where Christ is worshipped, and where men and women bow their knees to him.

## ONLY GOD KNOWS OUR HEARTS

Many Christians seem casual about their faith. We must not judge others. Life is hard, and only God sees our hearts. All humans are flawed and so are all churches. People who go to church know, on some level, they need help. The story is told of a man who wrote to a newspaper wondering why he should go to church. He wrote, "I've gone to church for thirty years, and in that time I've heard about three thousand sermons. But for the life of me I can't remember a single one of them in its entirety. I think I'm wasting my time, and the pastors are wasting theirs by giving sermons."

This started a controversy in the letters-to-the-editor column which went on for weeks, until someone wrote: "I've been married for thirty years. In that time my wife has cooked about thirty-two thousand meals. But for the life of me I cannot recall the entire menu for a single one of them. But I do know this, they all nourished me and gave me the strength I needed to do my work. If my wife had not given me these meals, I would be physically dead today. Likewise, if I had not gone to church for nourishment, I would be spiritually dead today!"

Many Christians who appear casual have been nourished just by being in the holy atmosphere of worship and the church community. God works slowly and gently in the lives of most of us. As we talk of transforming our lives and our churches, we need to guard against judging others. God's ways are not our ways (Isa. 55:8).

## GOD'S PROVIDENCE

God's providence surprised us throughout our faith journey. In hindsight, his guiding hand is obvious and amazing. He led us to three marvelous (yet imperfect) churches. Each one was just right for us at the time he took us there. His timing is perfect! God led us to Main Street Church and to Wesley, whom he used to teach us about his love, to heal my childhood wounds, to gently change our worldview, and to thrust us into leadership. He also used us at Main Street in the leadership of the Counseling Center and the Third Option—way beyond our dreams.

God led Jim to Main Street Church to show us loss is sometimes gain and to challenge us to be bolder—to reach out with hugs and help. God used Jim to give us a thirst for in-depth Bible studies and to encourage us to more prayer. God sent Jim to enhance our worship with Communion at the kneeling rail, so we would humble ourselves and welcome his presence.

God even gave us Edna! He sent Edna to teach us to recognize false teaching, to shake us loose from Main Street Church and from our comfortable small town. I never wanted to pray the prayer of Jabez.[2] I had enough territory. But God expanded our territory anyway. He does have a mind of his own. Only someone like Edna could have shaken us loose from Main Street Church.

God thrilled us by leading us to an American Baptist church, the denomination I grew up in and my Dad's denomination, which he loved and served for fifty years. At Hillcrest Church we worshiped with our son and daughter-in-law and their two children, blessing and deepening these relationships. God used Hillcrest to expand our biblical knowledge and our outreach experiences. He used devout Christians to teach and mentor us and to further our Christian worldview. And he used us at Hillcrest to organize and lead the Third Option group for couples.

God surprised us again, leading us away from Hillcrest to a totally different church. Leaving Hillcrest and searching again was a painful but valuable experience. Grace Church has expanded our learning and growing in major ways. Our grasp of Scripture, our faith in the providence of God, and our knowledge of the postmodern church has been enlarged and enriched by the teaching at Grace Church.

Each of our three churches has been more unified and the congregation more biblically knowledgeable than the one preceding it. God is charting our growth path. We would not have been ready for Hillcrest Church before 2001 or for Grace Church before 2008. We needed more Bible study (Mike in Bible Study Fellowship), and we needed to grow in our marriage through the Third Option and marriage retreats. Readers who are struggling about leaving a church or finding another church should seek God's will. He has a plan for you, too. Listen and follow him. Stay where you are unless he clearly leads you elsewhere.

## Are You in Christ?

Do you know Christ? If you are not certain about your salvation, pray to receive Christ. Confess your sins to God and ask Jesus to come into your heart. Call your pastor and talk with him after you do this. Commit yourself to Christ and his church in a deeper way than ever before. We all need to recommit ourselves to Christ daily. We need to be new creations in Christ. We need to be transformed. Mark Driscoll says, "You can be baptized in the church, marry in the church, die in the church, and have your funeral in the church, and still wake up in hell if you are merely in the church and not in Christ."[3]

## Transforming Churches

In chapter 13 I described the Vineyard pastor who was fed up with "pansy" churches or "sissy" churches. The French word for pansy is *pensèe* and means thought. Pansies have three leaves and resemble a human face. They bend forward as though in deep thought. The American Secular Union and the Freedom from Religion Foundation use a pansy as a symbol to represent free thought. Isn't that interesting? Perhaps "pansy church" is a fitting title for churches that adapt to our secular culture—churches that value "free thought" over biblical thought.

What will it take to transform "sissy" or "pansy" churches? What will it take to transform casual Christians into captive Christians? It requires the Lily of the Valley; it requires Jesus Christ. He changes us. The lily of the valley is linked to Jesus in Scripture. "I am a rose of Sharon, a lily of the valleys" (Song 2:1). "I will be like the dew to Israel; he will blossom like a lily" (Hos. 14:5). The lily is fragrant, pure white, and beautiful, as is our Lord and Savior. In order to not be pansy churches, we must become Lily of the Valley churches, sold out to him.

Ideally, the local church comforts and challenges us, supports and stretches us, touches us tenderly, and teaches us tenaciously. Ideally, the church guides us in gentleness and guards us in greatness, shows us his holiness and humbles us before him. Ideally, the church prepares us in prayer and prevents us from pride. It shows us our Savior and also our sin. The church focuses our eyes upward to Christ and outward to our needy world. This is a tall order. When a church is unified and surrendered to Christ, his Holy Spirit will be able to work through it in this way. We don't do it. He does it.

## Our First Love Calls Us

Jesus said, "On this rock I will build my church" (Matt. 16:18). The rock referred to is Peter's recognition that Jesus is the Christ, the Son of the living God. When the church is built on him and his Word, it will be a transforming church. We don't transform ourselves, he does it. The local church loses its spark when it abandons its first love. In Revelation 1:20–3:1, John has an incredible vision of the Lord Jesus Christ moving among the seven golden lampstands (churches).

Jesus addresses each of the seven churches. The church at Ephesus left its first love. The church at Pergamum accepted false doctrines. The church at Thyatira allowed immorality among them. The church at Sardis was dead. The church at Laodicea was lukewarm. Two of the seven churches did not receive criticism. The church at Smyrna endured persecution and didn't know its richness. The church at Philadelphia kept his Word and didn't deny his name—was faithful.

Church members, where are you among these churches? Have you left your first love, or does your heart warm within you at the mention of his name? Have you accepted false doctrines, or are you holding to the Truth of his Word? Are you lukewarm, neither hot nor cold? Or are you on fire for the Lord? Are you living in an immoral way? Or are you keeping the standards of purity and holiness he has set for us? Is your faith dead? Are you just going through the motions? Turn to Jesus and repent. We each need to examine our hearts daily, recognize our sin and failure, and seek his forgiveness. We need to seek him with all our heart. Then the church will be on fire. We need to be humble and willing to face persecution for him, as the church at Smyrna did. We need to keep his Word and not deny his name, as the church at Philadelphia did.

## The Church Universal

Early in our return to church, we attended a very inspiring inter-denominational worship service at another church. We saw friends from all over town. It thrilled and surprised me to realize I had brothers and sisters in Christ scattered in other churches through out my town. I now know I have brothers and sisters in Christ all over the world! Though we are scattered in many denominations, and though we have some differences, we are still one in Christ. Let this thought thrill you as it does me.

Joshua Harris echoes my thoughts.

> Please don't take Sunday for granted. Do whatever it takes to rediscover the wonder of it all. Next Sunday, during the morning service, look around and remind yourself: *These are my blood-bought brothers and sisters in Christ. We are His church, His people. We are here this morning to proclaim His work in our lives. We are here to give witness to the world of His great love and power and glory.*[4]

## JESUS' PRAYER FOR THE CHURCH

Before Christ's death he prayed for the church through the ages, including us, saying, "I pray … for those who will believe in me through their [the disciples'] message, that all of them may be one, Father, just as you are in me and I am in you. May they also be in us so that the world may believe that you have sent me. I have given them the glory that you gave me, that they may be one as we are one: I in them and you in me. May they be brought to complete unity to let the world know that you sent me and have loved them even as you have loved me" (John 17:20–23).

> Gracious heavenly Father,
> You are holy, holy, holy. You are Lord of Lords and King of Kings. You are the Lily of the Valley. Use us as channels for your transforming love, so the world may know that Jesus Christ is Lord, and the church is his bride. In his precious name we pray. Amen.

# ACKNOWLEDGMENTS

I THANK GOD for my life in Christ and for his inspiration for this book. I thank God for the churches and pastors described here and for the churches and pastors of my youth.

I thank my prayer team—my family, friends and small groups who prayed and encouraged me through the writing and publication of this book. I thank my technology team—my sons and daughter-in-law. I thank my sweet husband for his patience, love, help and encouragement throughout.

I thank the friends and family members who read all or part of my manuscript and offered valuable comments and support. Thanks to Adrien, Alice and Tom, Allison, Betty, Carol, Diane, Grant, Jim, Jon, Joni, Lola and Marv, Marion, Paula and Larry, Steve and the elders, and Wayne.

Many of you worshiped with Mike and me at one of the three churches described in this book. All of you are brothers and sisters in Christ and have played a significant role in my life. Words are inadequate. All I can say is, "I thank my God every time I remember you" (Phil. 1:3).

# Endnotes

## Part 1: A Journey in Three Churches

1. Brad Waggoner, "Study of Adults who Switch Churches: Why They Flee," *LifeWay Research* 2006: *www.lifeway.com.*

## Chapter 1: A Faith Journey

1. "Paganism at the Re-Imagining Conference 1993," *Brethren Revival Fellowship*, editorial, May/June 1994, Volume 29, Number 3, www.brfwitness.com, posted April 22, 2009.

## Chapter 2: Strange Teachings

1. Julian of Norwich lived in the thirteenth century. She lived a life of prayer, contemplation, and counseling in a small cell attached to a church in Norwich, England. *www.julianofnorwich.com.*

## Chapter 4: A Big Surprise Church

1. American Baptist Church, Biennial Meeting Update: June 25, 2001, *www.abc-usa.org* (July 4, 2001).

### Interlude: Guide for Leavers and Leaders

1. Brad Waggoner, "Study of Adults Who Switch Churches: Why They Flee," *LifeWay Research* 2006: *www.lifeway.com.*
2. Thomas C. Oden, *Turning Around the Mainline: How Renewal Movements Are Changing the Church* (Grand Rapids: Mich., Baker Books, 2006), 16.
3. Michael S. Hamilton and Jennifer McKinney, "Turning the Mainline Around," *Christianity Today*, August 2003, *www.christianitytoday*.com (April 30, 2010).
4. Mark Dever, *Nine Marks of a Healthy Church,* (Wheaton, Ill.: Crossway Books, 2004), 197–198.
5. Beth Moore, *The Patriarchs: Encountering the God of Abraham, Isaac and Jacob* (Nashville: Lifeway Press, 2005), 15.

### Chapter 8: Ideas for the Sheep

1. John Piper, *Desiring God: Meditations of a Christian Hedonist* (Sisters, Oregon: Multnomah 1996), 139.
2. John MacArthur, *The Anatomy of a Church*, (Panorama City, Calif.: Word of Grace Communications, Moody Press Edition, 1986), 3.
3. Charles Haddon Spurgeon, *The Sword and the Trowel*, 1888 complete volume, iii.

### Chapter 9: Ideas for the Shepherds

1. John Stott, *The Contemporary Christian* (Downers Grove, Ill.: InterVarsity Press, 1992), 281.
2. Calvin Miller, *Life is Mostly Edges: A Memoir* (Nashville: Thomas Nelson, 2008), 177.
3. John Stott, *The Contemporary Christian*, 286–287.
4. David Wilkerson, "Whatever Happened to Repentance Preaching?" *Pulpit Series Newsletters*, January 15, 2007, www.worldchallenge.org.

5. Rick Warren, *The Purpose Driven Church: Growth Without Compromising Your Message & Mission*, (Grand Rapids, Mich.: Zondervan Publishing House, 1995), 183.
6. Gordon MacDonald, *Who Stole My Church? What to Do When the Church You Love Tries to Enter the 21st Century* (Nashville: Thomas Nelson, 2007), 162–163.
7. Brad Waggoner, "Study of Adults Who Switch Churches: Why They Flee," LifeWay Research 2006: www.lifeway.com.

**Chapter 10: Worthy Worship**

1. Julia Duin, *Quitting Church: Why the Faithful Are Fleeing and What to Do about It* (Grand Rapids, Mich.: Baker Books, 2008), 68.
2. Charles Colson, "Musical Mush," posted February 6, 2006. *Breakpoint*, www.breakpoint.com.
3. Wayne Grudem, *Systematic Theology: An Introduction to Biblical Doctrine* (Grand Rapids, Mich.: Zondervan 2004), 42.
4. Kevin Twit, "Why Hymns?" Worship.Com, www.worship.com.
5. Terry Teykl, *The Presence Based Church* (Muncie, Ind.: Prayer Point Press, 2003), 204.
6. Julia Duin, *Quitting Church,* 69, 76–77, 78.
7. Charles R. Swindoll, *The Church Awakening: An Urgent Call for Renewal* (New York, NY, Hachette Book Group, 2010) 239–240.
8. David F. Wells, *The Courage to Be Protestant: Truth-lovers, Marketers, and Emergents in the Postmodern World* (Grand Rapids, Mich., Wm. B. Eerdmans Publishing Co., 2008), 231.
9. Mark Driscoll and Gerry Breshears, *Vintage Church: Timely Truths and Timely Methods* (Wheaton, Ill.: Crossway Books, 2008), 102.

10. Joshua Harris, *Stop Dating the Church: Fall in Love with the Family of God* (Colorado Springs, Colo.: Multnomah Publishers, 2004), 111.
11. Matt Redman, *Face Down* (Ventura, Calif.: Regal Books, 2004), 87.
12. Terry Teykl, *The Presence Based Church*, 36.
13. D. A. Carson, Editor, *Worship by the Book*, "Reformed Worship in the Global City" by Timothy J. Keller (Grand Rapids, Mich.: Zondervan, 2002), 229.
14. Rick Warren, *The Purpose Driven Church: Growth Without Compromising Your Message and Mission* (Grand Rapids, Mich.: Zondervan, 1995), 265–266.

**Chapter 11: Christ-like Makeovers**

1. Jim Cymbala, *Fresh Wind, Fresh Fire: What Happens When God's Spirit Invades the Hearts of His People* (Grand Rapids, Mich.: Zondervan Publishing House, 1997), 160.
2. John MacArthur, *The Anatomy of a Church* (Chicago, Ill., Moody Press, 1986), 72.
3. Joshua Harris, *Stop Dating the Church: Fall in Love with the Family of God* (Colorado Springs, Colo.: Multnomah Publishers, 2004), 94.
4. Neil T. Anderson and Charles Mylander, *Extreme Church Makeover: A Biblical Plan to Help Your Church Achieve Unity and Freedom in Christ* (Ventura, Calif.: Regal Books, 2005), 23.
5. Neil T. Anderson and Charles Mylander, *Extreme Church Makeover*, 12.

**Chapter 12: Go and Tell, Go and Help**

1. John Piper, *Let the Nations Be Glad* (Grand Rapids, Mich., Baker Books, 1993), 11.

2. Mark Dever, *Nine Marks of a Healthy Church* (Wheaton, Ill.: Crossway Books, 2004), 133.
3. Dan Kimball, *They Like Jesus but Not the Church: Insights from Emerging Generations* (Grand Rapids, Mich.: Zondervan, 2007), 168–169.
4. D.A. Carson, Editor, *Telling the Truth: Evangelizing Postmoderns,* Don Bartel, "Evangelizing Postmoderns Using a Mission Outpost Strategy" (Grand Rapids, Mich.: Zondervan, 2007), 345.
5. D.A. Carson, Editor, *Telling the Truth*, Susan Hecht, "Faithfully Relating to Unbelievers in a Relational Age," 249.
6. Dan Kimball, *They Like Jesus but Not the Church,* 166–167 (Visuals 173, 179–181).
7. D. A. Carson, Editor, *Telling the Truth,* Susan Hecht, "Faithfully Relating to Unbelievers in a Relational Age," 247.
8. Jason Mandryk, *Operation World* (Colorado Springs, Colo., Biblica Publishing, 2010).

**Chapter 13: Changing Churches in a Changing Culture**

1. Leonard Sweet, *SoulTsunami: Sink or Swim in New Millennium Culture* (Grand Rapids, Mich.: Zondervan, 1999), back cover.
2. Eric Gorski, The Associated Press, "Megachurch attendance skews younger," *Cincinnati Enquirer*, June 10, 2009, A6.
3. Michael Horton, *Christless Christianity: The Alternative Gospel of the American Church* (Grand Rapids, Mich.: Baker Books, 2008), 227.
4. "What Reveal Reveals," *a Christianity Today* editorial posted February 27, 2008, *www.christianitytoday.com.*
5. Leonard Sweet, *The Gospel According to Starbucks: Living with a Grande Passion* (Colorado Springs, Colo.: Waterbrook Press, 2007), 60.

6. Peter Scazzero, *The Emotionally Healthy Church: A Strategy for Discipleship That Actually Changes Lives* (Grand Rapids, Mich.: Zondervan, 2010), 141.
7. Mark Driscoll and Gerry Breshears, *Vintage Church: Timely Truths and Timely Methods* (Wheaton, Ill.: Crossway Books, 2008), 146.
8. Stuart Briscoe, "Walking with God for the Long Haul" Billy Graham Training Center, September 21–23, 2009, from Briscoe's talks on CDs.
9. *Christianity Today*, editorial on *Time* magazine's Person of the Year 2006, posted January 2007, *www.christianitytoday.com*.
10. Chuck Colson, *Against The Night: Living in the New Dark Ages* (Ann Arbor, Michigan: Servant Books, Fellowship Communications 1989), 98.
11. Nancy Pearcey, *Total Truth: Liberating Christianity from Its Cultural Captivity* (Wheaton, Ill.: Crossway Books, 2004), 240.
12. Chuck Colson, *The Body: Being Light in Darkness* (Dallas: Word Publishing, 1992), 188.
13. Michael Horton, *Christless Christianity*, 114.
14. Mark Driscoll, *Religion Saves: And Nine Other Misconceptions* (Wheaton, Ill.: Crossway Books 2009), 210.
15. Kevin DeYoung & Ted Kluck, *Why We're Not Emergent* (Chicago, Ill.: Moody, 2008), 194.
16. Mark Driscoll and Gerry Breshears, *Vintage Church*, 55.
17. George Barna, "Casual Christians and the Future of America," May 22, 2009, *www.barna.org*.

**Chapter 14: Transforming Churches**

1. Michelle Weiner-Davis, *Fire Your Shrink: Do-It-Yourself Strategies for Changing Your Life and Everyone in It* (New York: Simon and Shuster, 1995), 86.

2. *The Prayer of Jabez* by Bruce Willkinson challenged Christians to ask God to "enlarge their territory" (their influence or mission) as Jabez did in 1 Chronicles 4:9–10.
3. Mark Driscoll and Gerry Breshears, *Vintage Church: Timely Truths and Timely Methods* (Wheaton, Ill.: Crossway Books, 2008), 43.
4. Joshua Harris, *Stop Dating the Church: Fall in Love with the Family of God* (Colorado Springs, Colo.: Multnomah Publishers, 2004), 118.

CPSIA information can be obtained at www.ICGtesting.com
Printed in the USA
BVOW022130110312

284894BV00001B/18/P

9 781414 121529